MISSISSIPPI VALLEY ARCHITECTURE

Houses of the Lower Mississippi Valley

by Stanley Schuler

Schiffer Publishing Ltd

Other books by Stanley Schuler available from Schiffer Publishing Ltd.

The Cape Cod House
Coal Heat
American Barns

Forthcoming book:
Survey of New England Architecture

These books may be purchased from the publisher. Please include $1.50 postage. Try your bookstore first.

Library of Congress Catalog Number: 83–51744

Printed in the United States of America.
ISBN: 0-916838-96-X
Published by Schiffer Publishing Ltd., Box E, Exton, Pennsylvania 19341

PREFACE

My definition of the Lower Mississippi Valley is strictly arbitrary and limited: The Valley extends from below New Orleans to St. Louis in a swath that rarely reaches more than 100 miles east or west of the river. I know the area well and love it. The greater part of my family has lived there for generations. I have traveled it back and forth in all directions; visited it regularly for many, many years; lived there while writing another book.

The great majority of the 274 houses in this book are on the National Register of Historic Places. I selected them—and the equally fine unlisted homes—not just because of their outstanding beauty. (Some are quite plain; a couple are downright homely.) Rather, I wanted to show a cross-section of interesting houses—all the fine Valley houses, large and small, important and unimportant, that give a rounded picture of Valley architecture.

Furthermore, as the opening paragraph makes clear, I've included houses in the Valley states that have generally been overlooked. This is because the houses at the northern end of the Valley have a definite kinship with those closer to the Gulf of Mexico. Most reporters of the architectural scene have pretty well ignored this fact.

Ideally, I should have arranged the book so that houses of the same general style were grouped. This would have emphasized the point that northern Valley houses are linked architecturally to southern ones. But for one simple reason I have foiled my own good intentions by grouping houses by state. This is not a travel or guide book. But I feel sure it's a book that travelers interested in houses will use; and it will be more useful to them if they don't have to hunt through two-hundred-odd pages to find all the interesting houses in, say, eastern Arkansas. This arrangement also helps the person who wants to sort out and study the houses in his or her home state.

Most of the photographs I have used I took myself. If some seem a bit hazy or cheerless, blame the weather. It's easy to blame the weather for almost anything, but Valley weather in February and March 1982 was not kind to picture-takers. The remaining excellent shots were supplied by the following:

Arkansas Historic Preservation Program—Pages 165 (bottom), 173 (bottom), 176.

Jack E. Boucher for the Historic American Buildings Survey—Pages 88 (bottom), 89 (bottom), 96 (top), 97.

Collections of the Library of Congress—Pages 22 (bottom), 99, 100, 102 (bottom), 108, 109, 110, 111, 119 (bottom), 132 (top), 142 (bottom), 151 (bottom).

Mary Wallace Crocker (three of these pictures were also used in Mrs. Crocker's book, *Historic Architecture of Mississippi*)—Pages 23 (bottom), 71, 96 (bottom), 190.

James K. Mellow for the National Trust for Historic Preservation—Page 140.

Mississippi Department of Archives and History—Pages 36, 37 (bottom), 44 (top), 45, 52, 53, 54 (bottom, 55 (bottom), 59.

Missouri Botanical Garden—Page 200 (top and bottom right)

William J. Naeger—Pages 216, 217, 218, 219, 224 (top and bottom left), 227 (top).

Piaget (these pictures were taken for Charles van Ravenswaay's book, *German Houses in Missouri*)—Pages 209, 210, 211, 212.

State of Illinois Department of Conservation—Page 214.

Photographs taken for historical and promotional purposes were provided by the owners of several homes.

Stanley Schuler

Houses of the
LOWER MISSISSIPPI VALLEY

The history of the white man's exploration and colonization of the Mississippi Valley is checkered and confusing.

The Spanish started the parade, seeking gold to no avail. Cabeza de Vaca was probably the first white man to see the Mississippi River, though only the mouth of the river. That was in 1528. Thirteen years later, after trekking all over the South, Hernando DeSoto crossed the river in the vicinity of Memphis, journeyed on westward and then southward, and returned to the river where he died. His bones probably lie in Louisiana about opposite Natchez. Luis de Moscoso then took over DeSoto's expedition, built boats and led what was left of the men down river to its mouth.

Now came the French—first from Canada, then from the Gulf of Mexico. Pierre Esprit Radisson reached the upper Mississippi in 1654. In 1673, Louis Jolliet and Pere Marquette descended the river to below where DeSoto had crossed. Nine years later, the great adventurer and visionary, Robert Cavalier, Sieur de LaSalle, went down the river to its mouth, claimed all the territory drained by it, and named this Louisiana in honor of Louis XIV.

Up to that time no attempt to settle the Valley had been made. It was not until 1699 that a mission was established by Quebec priests. It was across the Mississippi from what is now St. Louis and was called Cahokia. In the same year Pierre Lemoyne d'Iberville, heading an expedition from France, established a fort at what is now Ocean Springs, Mississippi. Nothing that was originally built in either place remains today. The fort was abandoned within a few years, after disease and hunger virtually wiped out the men. It took Cahokia some 20 years to become prosperous; but eventually it too was virtually abandoned because of flooding.

Nevertheless, the two tiny communities were a start. The French established Kaskaskia in southern Illinois in 1703 (it was later washed away by a flood); Nachitoches (pronounced *Nak*-uh-tush) in western Louisiana in 1713; Fort Rosalie at Natchez in 1716 (this was wiped out by the Natchez Indians and the town did not really come into existence until 1768, under the British); New Orleans in 1718; Ste. Genevieve, Missouri, on the banks of the Mississippi, somewhere between 1723 and 1735.

The French held sway in the Valley until 1762. But from that time on for forty years many of the people who migrated to the area must have been unsure to which country they owed allegiance.

In 1762 France ceded the vast Louisiana territory to Spain. A year later Spain transferred all the area east of the Mississippi, except the Isle of Orleans, to England. Later Spain reconquered this area. Still later, most of the area was transferred to the new United States government. Then, in 1800, Spain returned the area west of the Mississippi to France. Finally, in 1803, the United States bought it.

The domestic architecture of the Lower Mississippi Valley stems in part from these many changes in territorial ownership. When people move to a strange and unpopulated land, they tend to take with them the architecture they are accustomed to; and to considerable extent, that happened in the Valley.

But since Spanish rule of the Louisiana Territory was short-lived and since there never were a great many Spaniards living there, their impact on Valley houses was slight, almost illusory. They built nothing similar to the boxy, fortress-like homes that their cousins put up in the Southwest and California. In fact, except for several public buildings in New Orleans, their contribution to Lower Mississippi Valley architecture is limited to such things as brick flooring at ground level, small shuttered windows and arched passageways for carriages to pass through a house.

English rule had even less impact. After all, the great majority of the English who came to the Valley after 1763 were American Colonials who migrated from the Eastern Seaboard, and such architectural preferences as they brought with them were American rather than English.

But the influence of the French is unmistakable and has continued even to this day. French architecture entered the Valley from the north, via Canada, and from the south, via the West Indies. In the public mind it is most pronounced in New Orleans. But it is no less pronounced in the little town of Ste. Genevieve. The houses in one area are much like those in the other, indicating their common ancestry. They are low, have steep hip roofs, and in the earliest days had walls built of mud, bricks or stones crammed between closely spaced posts.

The same style of house had been built in Normandy many years earlier. Yet the French-style houses of the Lower Mississippi Valley differ decidedly from their Norman predecessors. This difference, it is often said, traces to the fact that the West Indies were for many Frenchmen a way-station on the road to Louisiana. There may be some truth in this. Since the climate of southern Louisiana and Mississippi is roughly comparable to that of the Caribbean islands, the devices used by Frenchmen in the islands to combat the sun and heat—notably the galleries and one-room-deep floor plans—may well have been taken to the mainland. But this hardly explains why the same ideas were used 600 miles north in Ste. Genevieve unless the Ste. Genevievians that carried furs and other goods down river in flat boats and keel boats brought the ideas back north from New Orleans.

No, while the French Colonial architecture of the Lower Mississippi Valley was probably influenced by the West Indies, it derived primarily from something else: The climate. The topography. And the availability and unavailability of building materials.

Although the French Colonial style of architecture—some call it the Creole style—is prevalent in the Lower Mississippi Valley (in some areas more than in others), it is not dominant.

Among houses built before the War between the States—which is, with some exceptions, the cut-off date for the houses shown in this book—there is no dominant style. That's one of the things that makes houselooking so pleasurable in the Valley.

In architecture, as in almost everything else, there are fads. And even though French Colonial architecture was peculiarly well suited to the Valley, it gave way to the Greek Revival style when that swept the country in the period from roughly 1820 to 1860.

Then came Victorian—as elsewhere in the fast-developing nation.

Intermingled with the houses of these three easily identifiable styles are others that have no definite style. Architectural historians lump them under the heading of "vernacular architecture".

Vernacular may be defined as "of the people". One dictionary, referring specifically to architecture, defines it as "native or peculiar to popular tastes". Since all architecture has roots in the past, a vernacular house has stylistic features that are traceable to earlier architectural styles but it is an amalgam of old styles mixed with each builder's own ideas. Thus it is a concoction—a little bit of this, a little bit of that, a little bit of who-knows-what.

Some concoctions—whether of food, language or architectural styles—are good. Some are bad. The vernacular houses built in the Lower Mississippi Valley prior to 1860 are both; but by and large they are pleasing and often very attractive. They are also likely to be very livable and—unlike houses of a definite style such as Greek Revival—quite individualistic.

Since the Lower Mississippi Valley, as I have defined it, is roughly 650 miles long and incorporates four climate zones, one can hardly expect it to be homogeneous in character. Yet it has certain important common features.

The land is low; flat to gently undulating; and being laced by four great rivers—the Mississippi, Missouri, Ohio and Arkansas—and other large ones, it is subject to serious flooding.

The summers are long and hot (actually hotter, though shorter, at the northern end of the Valley than at the southern end).

Humidity is high. Rainfall ranges from moderate in Missouri to heavy in Louisiana.

The soil is deep, rather heavy and, in much of the area, free of stone.

In pioneer days, the entire country was densely forested and even today, when enormous acreage has been cleared for agriculture, the woodlands are vast and thick with pines, cypresses, oaks and other hardwoods.

These features of the Valley have always contributed substantially to Valley architecture, but they contributed most in the 1700s and early 1800s—before more sophisticated architectural styles and "better" building methods and products came into use.

A low, hot, humid country subject to flooding. Climate affected Lower Mississippi Valley homes in a way that verges on the unique.

For one thing, houses were raised well off the ground so that flood waters and hurricane-whipped waves along the Gulf Coast would do minimum damage; to provide an air space that would help to protect the houses and occupants from the dampness in the soil; and simply to get everyone up high enough to feel whatever breezes might be stirring. It is more than likely that houses were also raised so the owners could enjoy a better view over the flat countryside; but if this was a consideration, it was of minor importance.[1]

Because of the elevation of the first floor, houses of French Colonial design have come to be known as "raised cottages". (Since you cannot call a mansion a cottage, it is referred to as "a house of the raised-cottage type"). How much they were raised seems to have been dictated as much by the size of the house as by climatic considerations. Generally—this is a very broad generalization—small houses were raised only two or three feet while larger

[1] Which today has been negated in many houses close to rivers by the levees, which have been raised so high that it is almost impossible to see over them.

ones were raised six to eight.[2] In small houses, particularly those built by the Cajuns in Louisiana, the piers were cypress logs. In other houses, they were made of triangular bricks that were covered with cement plaster to protect against deterioration.

Also to take advantage of cooling breezes, earliest houses were commonly only one room deep.[3] This permitted a constant flow of air through every room. Later, when a second line of rooms was added behind the first, air flow was maintained by providing wide openings—not just single doors—between the front and back rooms.

But Mississippi Valley settlers could not and did not stop there in their efforts to make their homes comfortable.

Ceilings were built unusually high in order to increase the volume of air around room occupants. By contrast with early New England houses with seven-foot ceilings, small houses in the Valley had ten-foot ceilings and in large houses ceiling height ranged from twelve to as much as twenty-two feet.[4] That this made the house difficult to heat in winter mattered little: summer comfort was more important than winter comfort. But today's high energy costs have caused many owners of old homes to view the high ceilings with jaundiced eye. Despite the South's enormous supply of relatively cheap gas, heating is expensive and air conditioning even more so.

High ceilings also made possible much taller windows and doors to admit the breezes. In some houses, larger windows were coupled with transoms that could be kept open when the louvered shutters (all windows and doors had outside shutters) were closed. In other houses, the windows extended from floor level or almost floor level to a foot or two below the ceiling. And in still other houses, the windows also served as doors. These were called jib windows. Typically, they were in three sections. The lowest section was made of wood in two equal-size panels hinged to swing inward like French doors. The two upper sections were glazed sash. The top one was fixed; the lower was counterbalanced and slid upward. Thus, when the middle sash was raised and the wood panels were swung open, a doorway roughly four feet wide and seven to eight feet high was created.[5]

Tall windows with very low sills or no sills at all are an obvious threat to life and limb if they open onto thin air. But in the Valley they don't. All open onto the long covered porches known as galleries.

Depending on the design of the house, galleries were on one, two, three or four sides and usually extended the full length of each wall. In the one or one-and-a-half-story French Colonial houses, there was a

[2] There is a story, probably apochryphal, that when Pierre Baillio was building the Kent plantation house in Alexandria, Louisiana, in 1796 he decided to go to New Orleans to buy furnishings. Before leaving, he started his slaves on construction of the brick piers supporting the house. He figured that the work would be completed by the time he returned. But he was delayed in the city and when he got back to Alexandria he found his slaves still building higher and higher.

[3] However, one-room-deep design cannot be attributed solely to the need for air flow: The same plan was used elsewhere—even in New England. In other words, it stemmed from European practice, which early American colonists tended to follow.

[4] High ceilings were followed by towering beds. Some have posts, which support a tester, close to 12 feet tall. It may correctly be assumed that this was to improve the proportions of the beds to the bedrooms. But such great height had a practical value, too: Door and window screens were unknown in early days; therefore to protect sleepers against insects—especially malaria and yellow-fever mosquitoes—beds were swathed in fine-mesh cotton net, which reduces air circulation. Higher bed posts permitted a larger netting area, hence more air.

[5] In a few of the largest houses, both sash slid upward into a pocket in the wall.

gallery at the level of the main floor, and the roof of the house extended out over it in an unbroken sweep. (The rafters were carried on slender gallery columns—colonettes—centered over heavier columns supporting the gallery floor.) If the house was raised high enough off the ground for a man to stand upright under it, there was also usually a brick-floored gallery more or less at ground level beneath the upper gallery.

Since houses of later design were raised only a few feet off the ground, the first gallery in these was raised to the level of the main floor; and in two-story houses there was another gallery at the level of the second floor. (One of the things distinguishing a gallery from an ordinary porch is that it is always a continuation of the floor indoors.)

Galleries were not mere places to sit and rock. Of foremost importance, they kept all but the rising and setting sun off windows, doors and walls (which were uninsulated) and thus contributed to the relative coolness of the house. In like fashion, they shielded the walls, which were often made of mud, against rain.

They served as the halls, or corridors, by which the occupants of the house could pass from one room to another without going through one in between. This was made possible by the fact that, in large houses at least, every room had a door or jib window opening onto a gallery. Thus there was no need for interior halls (although these were generally used from the Greek Revival period on). Inside stairs were also unnecessary since galleries on different levels were connected by stairs.

Finally, because of the galleries, rooms could be added or subdivided without major reconstruction.[6] The common way to make a small addition was simply to enclose a section of a gallery.[7] Larger additions were usually made by building a wing with its own galleries connected to the galleries of the original house. Big rooms were equally easy to divide into small rooms without affecting traffic circulation through the house because the galleries served as the connecting links.

Rainfall ranges from moderate to heavy. To what extent rainfall affected roof design on the early houses in the Lower Mississippi Valley is hard to say. The steep hip roofs were a direct copy of earlier French roofs. But it's likely that the colonists would have switched to another simpler design, such as the gable roof, if the hip roof had not been so well suited to the Valley climate. For one thing, it shed water rapidly. This was important at the southern end of the Valley, where rainfall averages close to 60 inches a year. It was equally important at the northern end of the Valley where roofs were for a long time thatched with straw.

Another advantage of the hip roof was that it was an extremely efficient collector of the rainwater that was used for drinking, cooking and bathing. The roof was a rectangular umbrella over the always rectangular house. At the eaves it had no breaks or gaps. As a result, the wood gutters formed a continuous line all the way around the house and were sloped so that they carried all the water that fell onto the roof into one or two huge cisterns at the back or side of the house.

The soil is heavy and free of stone; the area heavily forested. The Europeans settling the New World were amazed at the dense forests and great trees they found; therefore it was not surprising—especially since they had to cut trees to create house

[6] Gallery width varied considerably. They were rarely less than six feet wide and, on larger houses, often were about twice that. In this respect, they differed from the balconies on houses in closely built-up areas such as New Orleans' French Quarter. Since balconies were shallow they were rarely converted into enclosed spaces. But they otherwise served the same purposes as galleries.

[7] This is a favorite method used by modern owners to add bathrooms.

sites—that they built their first homes of wood. Later, it's true, the wealthier colonists tended to switch to brick or stone because it was more permanent. But in the Lower Mississippi Valley, wood continued to be the favorite building material.

The Valley people's liking for wood might not have been so strong if it had not been for the area's peculiarities. First, stone was in most areas virtually non-existent. The only stone suitable for building—limestone—is so deeply covered by water-and wind-borne soil (loess) that in early days it was impractical to quarry.

Happily, the heavy soil was ideal for brickmaking. Many of the plantation owners set up their own kilns. But the bricks were not ideal for building because they were soft and tended to crumble after long exposure to moisture. That is why they had to be plastered.

On the other hand, the soil was highly suitable for making bousillage. A mixture of clay and Spanish moss or straw, this was widely used for building the walls of French Colonial houses.

In the forests, however, the settlers found a material that more than made up for the lack of stone, softness of bricks and dissolvability of bousillage. It was the bald cypress—*Taxodium distichum.*

Valley settlers that came directly from Europe had never seen anything like the cypress; and even those from the Carolinas, where the tree grows, must have been astonished and delighted with the great cypress swamps found all the way up river to southeastern Missouri. Here was an excellent building material. The trees grew straight to well over a hundred feet and from three to as much as twelve feet in diameter at breast height. The wood was strong, only moderately hard, straight-grained and easy to work. Best of all, it had great resistance to the omnipresent decay organisms and termites. Small wonder that, despite the widespread availability of hard yellow pine and durable oak, cypress was used for everything from sills and joists to siding, roof shingles, flooring and the balustrades on galleries. Whole tree trunks were even used for the enormous columns of some houses such as Rosedown.

Small wonder, too, that so many of the old Valley homes are still standing. By the time the early builders got through fitting large cypress timbers together by joinery methods similar to those used by the colonists along the Eastern Seaboard, their houses could withstand not just the ordinary wear and tear of age but also humidity and insects and even floods and hurricanes. There was only one thing that could best them: fire. Fire has taken many of the plantation houses simply because they were and still are so far beyond the reach of fire departments. Among others, it destroyed Versailles more than half a century after the Battle of New Orleans had raged around it. It destroyed Windsor, near Port Gibson, Mississippi, leaving only twenty-two towering Corinthian columns. Just a little over twenty years ago, it destroyed Greenwood, the gorgeous Greek Revival mansion outside St. Francisville, Louisiana, that is still shown, partially reflected in a lake, on picture postcards.[8]

Several other things that were common to all parts of the Lower Mississippi Valley also influenced the design of early houses.

Partly because fire was an obvious menace, kitchens—even in cities—were generally in a building separate from the main house.

To provide a place for the young men of the family and their friends to cavort, another separate building called a garconniere was built. (In the city, however, the garconniere was usually in a wing of

[8] Greenwood has since been rebuilt; but with all due appreciation of the owners' efforts, it is not quite the house it was. In this day of staggering construction costs and indifferent workmanship, it is impossible to create out of plywood and two-by-fours what our ancestors built with thick, solid cypress.

the house.) On the plantations, this was commonly accompanied by yet another building, sometimes identical, called the pigeonniere. Here pigeons were raised on the second floor and school was kept on the first.

The land was vast. The picture on page 86 says this more eloquently than words. Looking at it, you can understand why plantation houses were often so enormous (there was no necessity for making them small); why they had no need of cellars for storage space; why they were surrounded by innumerable outbuildings. The basic fact is that, because of the availability of land, the plantation houses were far apart and even greater distances from towns; therefore each house had to be the focal point of its own miniature, more of less self-supporting community.

But outside of the natural characteristics of the Lower Mississippi Valley, the one thing that dictated the design of the houses was the plentitude of slave labor. Slaves were not peculiar to the South in our nation's early days. Close to where I live in Connecticut, a man named Brown owned 10,000 acres which were worked by over 40 slaves. Nevertheless, it is true that slavery to a southern farmer and also to a southern city merchant was a way of life. Slaves made it possible to keep the sizable homes going. More than that, without slaves, the houses could never have been built because, even if other labor had been available, the houses would have cost too much.

Were slaves capable of the joinery that gave lasting strength to Valley houses; of turning out the intricate capitals, beautiful moldings and ceiling centerpieces that adorn the houses? They must have been because it was not until shortly before the War between the States that city mills began to supply millwork. Prior to that time, the slaves—frequently under the direction of transient artisans—had to do virtually all the work themselves.

The earliest houses in the Lower Mississippi Valley were little better than huts (just as the first houses built by the Pilgrims at Plymouth were huts). It's doubtful that any remain. They fell down; were burned; or were washed away. But better houses came along fairly soon—also to disappear. Madame John's Legacy is thought to be the oldest house in New Orleans, having been put up in 1726. But it was burned down along with practically everything else in the city on Good Friday, 1788; and the house now standing dates from that year and is a duplicate of the original. The oldest houses in Natchez, Nachitoches and Biloxi date from the same period. As does the Saucier house at Cahokia. So unless there are some ancient houses hidden away in the countryside, "oldest" honors must go to those in Ste. Genevieve. But even here you find no certifiably original houses, because they were built on the big field—*le grand champ*—bordering the Mississippi, and the river destroyed them in 1785. However, a few of the community's residents evidently foresaw this catastrophe and either moved their houses to higher ground or built new ones before then. Some believe the Jean Baptists Valle house was built some time around 1762; the St. Gemme-Amoureux and Beauvais houses about 1770; the Bequette-Ribault house about 1775.

By this time the Louisiana territory had passed out of French hands. Even so, French architectural and building tradition remained strong, although it was considerably altered by the Valley's natural characteristics.

The great majority of the houses built before 1820 were one or one-and-a-half stories high. There were three general types, all French Colonial but far from alike: the large plantation houses and the small Cajun houses and Creole cottages. All of these are mainly associated with Louisiana, although the first and last were not restricted to that state and a number of houses in other parts of the Lower Mississippi Valley are akin to all three. For example, the houses in Ste. Genevieve were initially small-scale cousins of the raised, hip-roofed plantation house. But in some later period that cannot be pinpointed they underwent two changes that moved at least some of them into the Cajun and Creole house class: They were built closer to the ground and they acquired gable roofs extending over front and rear galleries. Just how many of those that now have gable roofs were actually built that way is uncertain. But examination of the structures indicates that in some cases the original hip roofs were converted into gable roofs in order to make the attics brighter, airier and more livable.

Cajun houses, constructed by the Frenchmen who were driven out of Acadia by the English in the middle 1700s, are limited to the southern Louisiana countryside. They were generally raised only about a foot off the ground and had gable roofs sloping front to back. The front half of the roof continued over the gallery, from which a very steep flight of stairs rose to the attic, which was used as a garconniere or loom room.

The first houses had only two rooms, one in front of the other. Later four rooms were clustered around the central chimney. Still later a few houses had three rooms across the front and two *cabinets* (small rooms or closets) in back at the ends of the house. Between the *cabinets* was a short gallery.

The principal distinguishing characteristic of Cajun houses is their simplicity. Although the bousillage side and rear walls were protected from the weather by siding, the front wall was not. Ornamentation was almost totally lacking (but more recent Cajuns seem to have developed a penchant for fancifully-cut balusters on the gallery).

Creole cottages are, at a glance, quite similar. They, too, were built close to the ground and had front-and-back-sloping gable roofs.[9] The Creole cottage, however, was a city house. It was set flush with the sidewalk and had no front gallery, but it did have a roof projecting over the sidewalk. In the earliest houses this overhang was cantilevered out from the facade, but later it became an unsupported extension of the house roof. In his memoires, the famous architect Benjamin Latrobe, who moved to New Orleans in 1820, noted that most of the houses of his day had steep roofs extending over the *banquettes* as much as five feet. The roofs, he said, were covered with Spanish tiles from the West Indies. This was because the city authorities, ruing the great fire of 1788 and another big though less serious one in 1794, had ruled that more fireproof materials must be used. (After 1800 slate replaced the tiles.) Elsewhere in the Valley, however, wood shingles were used until they gave way—many years later—to steel sheets.

Most Creole cottages had four bays; that is, four openings—a shuttered door and three shuttered windows—on the street side. There were two rooms in front and two in back, all of equal size and all serving as passageways since French Colonial homes did not have halls. Behind these, facing a patio, were two *cabinets* flanking a recessed gallery with stairs to the upper floor. The large rooms were heated by fireplaces that vented into two chimneys, one centered in the front roof slope near the ridge; the other in the rear slope. Lower in the two roof surfaces were pairs of dormers.

Your first impression of Creole cottages is that they were simple and undistinguished. Many are; but many others are well proportioned and charming—typically French in spirit. They were usually built of plastered brick or brick rubble tinted a soft color. They often had dentiled

[9] Some Creole cottages, however, had hip roofs. These were usually built on corner lots or were only two bays wide. The latter today are often referred to as maisonettes.

cornices. Dormer windows were likely to be flanked by pilasters and arched pediments (and later the upper window sash were rounded). The windows and doors in the facades frequently were topped with delicate fanlights.

Interiors varied also. Some were plain; some were ornamented and decorated, but always quietly. (This was also true of the other house types.) Walls were mostly plastered and stark white. Ceilings were made of dressed boards beaded like modern tongue-and-groove partition boards. The finest mantels were of box design (projecting from the wall like a large, shallow box) with pilasters at the corners and panels between and on the sides.[10] If the cypress millwork used for trim was not painted white, it was likely to be painted to resemble oak or some other wood with better color and a more distinctive grain than cypress. Such wood was called *faux bois.* Front doors were also treated in this fashion. Or sometimes wood as well as stone was painted to resemble marble—*faux marbre.*

But while external features such as these are interesting, the most interesting thing about the French Colonial houses is the way in which they were built. This goes straight back to France, although the Indians of Louisiana followed a roughly similar practice and may have reinforced in the minds of the early settlers—especially the Cajuns—the desirability of the practice.

Two construction methods were used in houses (and a third essentially similar but cruder method was used for outbuildings). In the *poteaux en terre* method, squared posts were set vertically in the soil and fastened together only at the top. The spaces between the posts were then filled. Only the earliest houses were built in this way and few are left. In the *poteaux sur solle* method, the posts were placed on sills resting on stone foundations or wood blocks. In both methods, the spaces between posts were filled either with small stones or bricks and mortar, or bousillage.

Bousillage was made by filling a pit with mud, Spanish moss or straw and, frequently, burned shells. This was mixed with the feet. It was then draped over wood crosspieces (*barreaux*) fitted between the posts and compressed to the thickness of the posts. By increasing the size of the posts or using double rows, the walls were sometimes made as much as two feet thick. In plantation houses, after the filling had dried, the walls were completely plastered for protection against moisture. The Cajuns, however, used cypress siding and covered only the side and rear walls.[11]

Bousillage was used only in walls on the lowest floor of a house. The upper walls were framed and covered with wood. (In the 1800s, when bricks replaced bousillage, they were generally used only in the lower walls. They, too, were plastered and occasionally the plaster was tooled to resemble ashlar.)

After 1820, Valley architecture began to change—slowly at first, then rapidly. Plantation houses acquired a full second story, center halls and interior stairs. City houses grew to two, three and even four stories and also acquired halls. And the shotgun house, which was only one room wide and three or more rooms deep, appeared.[12] Everywhere except in the Cajun houses simplicity gave way to increased ornamentation.

[10] In my opinion, Valley fireplaces are rarely notable. Perhaps because New Englanders had more use for fireplaces, they tended to design them more beautifully.

[11] In the earliest Cajun houses, tapering chimneys were also made of bousillage packed between four saplings placed at the corners.

[12] Shotgun houses were so-called because, if you fired a shotgun through the front door, the pellets would travel through the doors from room to room (there was no hall) without striking anything until they reached the rear wall.

The change resulted from the increasing wealth of the Valley. The planters grew rich as they expanded their cotton and sugar cane acreage; and the city merchants followed suit as produce and goods were barged up and down the Mississippi and its tributaries. The number of slaves brought in swelled.

When men grow rich, the first thing they do is to display their wealth in their homes. And in the Valley they put on a dazzling display. It was not just that they wanted to impress. Out in the country, where the plantation houses were isolated, a family's main contact with the world was made through the people they entertained. And entertainment meant putting up friends and acquaintances overnight even though the focal point of the entertainment might be only a dinner party or ball. So the houses had to grow in size to accommodate more guests (as well as big families).

This development coincided with the birth of the Greek Revival style of architecture. It was a style made to order for the wealthy—especially for the often crude, ambitious, self-made men who migrated into the Valley to wrest their fortunes out of land that was still largely a wilderness.

The Greek Revival style sprang mainly from Washington's and Jefferson's feeling that the newly born United States should have an architecture of its own—something expressing the monumentality, simplicity, dignity and purity of ancient Greek democracy and the Roman republic. Naturally, this new style did not take hold instantly. It developed gradually as all architectural styles do (witness the snail-like spread of today's Modern style). But by the time it began to sweep westward from the Eastern Seaboard, the people of the Lower Mississippi Valley were ready for it.

But the French Colonial tradition was still strong, the peculiarities of the land and climate and the availability of materials could not be ignored. So the Greek Revival houses of the Valley—even those designed by the exemplary Greek Revival architects who moved south: Latrobe, James Gallier, Sr., Charles Dakin and his brother James—differed from those built elsewhere in the developing nation.

A few of the houses, to be sure, were almost "pure" Greek Revival. But in most houses the galleries and balconies of earlier days were retained. As were jib windows and French casements and raised first floors.

In the cities, notably New Orleans, the lavish use of ornamental ironwork continued and, indeed, became even more elaborate. Just when the use of ironwork started is difficult to determine. But the 1795-99 reconstruction of the Cabildo, which housed the Spanish governing council, in all likelihood popularized the use. The Cabildo's balcony railing was nothing short of splendid.

The railing was made of wrought iron. All those of this period were. Most of them came from Spain or perhaps Mexico. They were delicate and graceful. But along about 1840 cast iron began to replace wrought; and while these railings were no less charming they were considerably more complicated and formed more of a screen.[13]

The ironwork, whether wrought or cast, confuses the picture of the houses. Superficially they look French. But if you go behind the ironwork, the characteristics of the Greek Revival style are unmistakeable. The doorways are monumental, usually with sidelights and rectangular transom lights. The windows are bold and capped with large lintels. The roofs, whether hipped or gabled, are low, often

[13] Few of the plantation houses have ironwork; and on many of those that do it often seems out of place. I refused to photograph perhaps the most famous example because it detracted so much from the lines of the house. But much of the trouble stemmed from the fact that it was painted brilliant green.

partially concealed by a parapet, often with small windows under the eaves.

And of course there were large columns—freestanding or applied to the facade. Up to a point, these were faithful to the ancient orders—Corinthian, Composite, Doric, Ionic and Tuscan. But as was true throughout the United States, Valley architects and builders had no hesitation about changing the proportions of the columns and the design of the capitals and entablatures.

This may not be obvious to the untrained eye. What is obvious is that, whereas in earlier days the columns from ground level to the first floor were large and those above were much smaller, the Greek Revival columns rose unbroken from ground level to the roof and the joists for the upper gallery were simply tied into them. More than almost anything else, these huge columns, carefully spaced across the front of a house and often around the sides and back, gave the Valley plantation houses their look of monumentality. For instance, even though the house itself is gone, the columns of Windsor leave you with the feeling that this was not a home; it was a temple.

But once again came change. It began creeping into the Lower Mississippi Valley shortly before the War between the States. The Victorian style shouldered the Greek Revival aside.

Andrew Jackson Downing, probably the most influential of the early proponents of Victorian design, stressed this style as ideal for non-urban homes. But the Valley planters were not listening. There are very, very few Victorian plantation houses. Victorian was for town and city dwellers. The latters' houses were no more beautiful or grotesque than those elsewhere in the country. Above all, they were almost totally uninfluenced by the factors that dictated the French Colonial homes and that were perpetuated in the Greek Revival homes. As seen today, they seem to be only a foil for these earlier houses.

This is far from begin a bad thing.

As a foil, the Victorian houses emphasize the beauty of the French Colonial and Greek Revival houses while adding their own peculiar charm to the surrounding world.

More important, they take the curse off Valley architecture. Because if you take a long, concentrated look at the early Valley homes, you find that your interest becomes jaded and you begin to complain, "Oh, that's just another French Colonial." Or "I've seen enough Greek Revival." But just before you reach the point of total satiation, you come upon a Victorian house or an unusual vernacular house and incipient boredom disappears.

And you leave the Lower Mississippi Valley thinking, "I must come back for another look."

Mississippi

1. Biloxi
2. Carrollton
3. Church Hill
4. Fayette
5. Gautier
6. Grenada
7. Holly Springs
8. Jackson
9. Natchez
10. North Carrollton
11. Pass Christian
12. Port Gibson
13. Redwood
14. Vicksburg
15. Woodville
16. Yazoo City

BILOXI - 1856

The Tullis-Toledano house is a sophisticated vernacular summer home on the Gulf of Mexico not too far from where the French built their first coastal settlement in 1699. An outside stair connects the two floors. The dormers are very attractive—much like those on other Valley homes of the same era.

901

GAUTIER - 1845

Oldfields (opposite) superimposes vernacular Greek Revival design on a common deep South plan. Although close to the shore, the house is on land high enough to escape flooding by hurricanes, and perhaps for this reason, it is only a few feet above the ground (the front gallery, however, is almost at ground level). On the shore side of the house, transoms above all the doors let in air even when the doors are shuttered against the southern sun.

BILOXI - 1852

Beauvoir is one of the most famous houses in the South because it was the home of Jefferson Davis after the War between the States. It is a large and beautiful raised dwelling of French Colonial design but displays the fine detailing of the Greek Revival period. The high ground floor is walled with lattice to let the breezes flow through, thus helping to keep the summer temperatures tolerable. The rooms, shown on the next page, have been changed little since the Davis family's time. The enormous entrance hall is decorated in cool colors that add to the real coolness resulting from the towering ceiling and the sweep of air through large doors and windows. Double-size doorways, as between the back parlor and family room (overleaf, bottom), contribute further to circulation of air.

BILOXI

The Old Brick House fronts on the bay that bends in behind the city and it backs close to the street. It is best known today as the Biloxi Garden Center, because it's the home of that organization. The brick gable ends extend above the canted roof and there are three nicely proportioned dormers on both sides, thus assuring a sweep of air through the upper story. The central doorways in front and back are of Greek Revival design, but the house as a whole is a vernacular structure. Two additional smaller doors open onto the gallery.

PASS CHRISTIAN

This house was built in the mid-1800s, somewhat later than that above. It faces directly on the Gulf, but unlike many of its Pass Christian and Biloxi neighbors, it survived Hurricane Camille because it stands on the highest ground in the town, has a low profile and was very sturdily built. To combat the sun and no-seeums, which penetrate even the finest wire mesh, the gallery has been permanently enclosed in blue heat-and glare-reducing glass and air conditioned. But except for the slender uprights between the Victorian posts, this improvement is unnoticeable from the street.

NATCHEZ - 1812

Auburn is dominated by a giant portico with Ionic columns and a Corinthian entablature. This preceded similar porticoes in Virginia and became a model for many Natchez home owners. The doorways on both levels are based on Palladian motifs and have unusual arched heads that rather suggest an ancient Egyptian headdress. The floor plan is also unusual and provides for more intimate family gatherings than most big-house plans. The stairway in the entrance hall is free-standing and tightly spiraled.

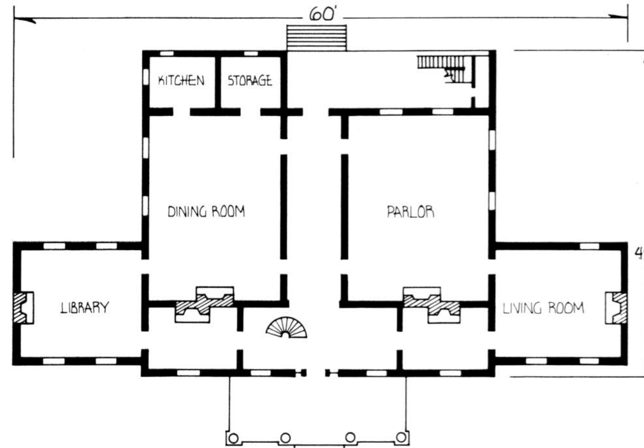

NATCHEZ - 1857

Frederick Stanton wanted the most palatial home in Natchez and he got it at great expense because he took pleasure in ornamenting Stanton Hall, inside and out, elaborately. He even imported many of the materials —the exterior ironwork and carved marble mantels from Italy; the Sheffield-silver hardware from England; the enormous gilt mirrors from France. Furthermore, he built at unusually grand scale even in a city noted for mansions. On both floors the house has great central halls flanked on either side by three rooms. The parlor, visually divided into two rooms by its ornate triple arch, can be combined with the music room behind it into a ballroom 72 feet long; and because of the mirrors on the walls, it appears larger.

NATCHEZ - 1840

D'Evereux is a Greek Revival temple fit for a goddess. It is perfectly proportioned outside (but the rooms are small). The front gallery is embellished with a little decorative-iron balcony overhanging the recessed entrance. At the back of the house there is a full second-story gallery. An enormous but well proportioned cupola ventilates the attic under the low hip roof.

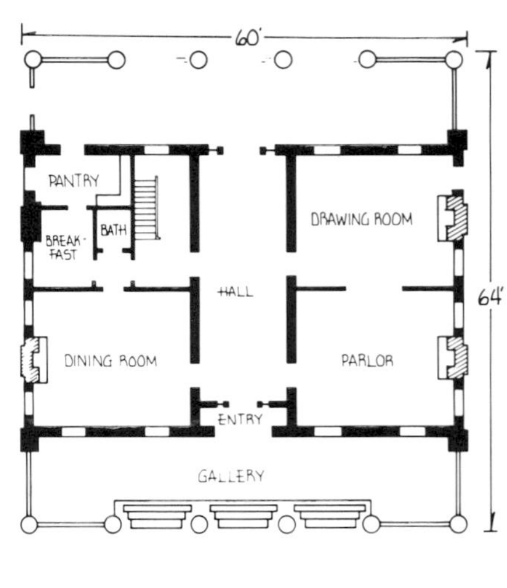

NATCHEZ - 1855

One of the effects of spacious double galleries, —especially when they surround a house on three sides, as here—is to make the house look much larger than its actual living space. Even so, Dunleith is hardly small. Downstairs on one side of the wide hall, which runs the depth of the house, are big double drawing rooms; on the other side, a library and dining room. On the second floor, similarly arranged, are four bedrooms; and the third floor has four more rooms. All the rooms have fireplaces.

NATCHEZ - 1836

Choctaw is a late but splendid example of the Neo-Classical style that was popular in Natchez at the turn of the Nineteenth Century. It stands large and high above the street in the downtown area. The great portico was largely for show. The owners lived in the summer on the double galleries that stretched the length of the house in the rear (shown at right).

NATCHEZ - 1810

Before Choctaw was built across the street, Cherokee (right) must have had a sweeping view of the river. Even now it sits so high above the street you almost pass it by. Don't. It's one of Natchez' earliest and best Greek Revival examples.

NATCHEZ - 1836

Green Leaves (below), another exemplary Greek Revival design, also sits high above the street and, in addition, is partly concealed by magnificent trees (especially an enormous live oak in the rear).

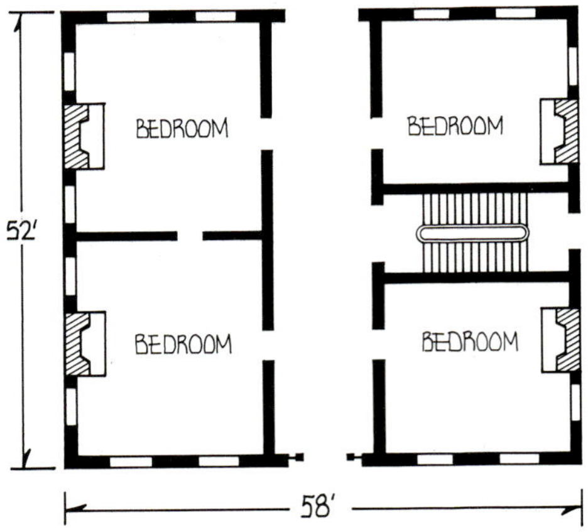

NATCHEZ

Except that the double galleries run the length of the house and there is a single dormer centered above the doors, the rear of Rosalie (1820) is like the front. (Pictured left; second-floor plan, above). Below is Texada (1805), probably Natchez' first brick building. It has also been a tavern, meeting place and shop. Built for a Spaniard, it has a Spanish feel. The second-story louvered gallery overlooks a rear courtyard.

NATCHEZ - 1855

Monteigne today bears no resemblance to the original house, which was an out-and-out Victorian structure with a one-story gallery on the front and sides. This was torn off and replaced by a classical portico in 1927. At the same time, the side galleries were enclosed in a classical manner. Some mourn the change but most rate the house, in its pink plaster dress, as one of the town's showplaces.

NATCHEZ - 1790

Evans-Bontura (right), also called Evansview, began life as a small two-story, one-room-deep, double-galleried house. Its Spanish origin is apparent in such things as an arched brick carriage-way running through the house. Then it was enlarged in 1830 and again in 1850. The last addition was the front brick structure, which resembles a transplanted New Orleans home.

NATCHEZ

Mount Repose (below) was built in 1824 and has remained in the same family. It is a splendid unrestored example of a Natchez-area plantation house. The roof, unlike some but not all, breaks where the galleries are

joined to the house. Mistletoe (opposite, top) was built in 1807 as a father's wedding present to a son. Twice enlarged, it still looks small, homey and unassuming outside, but it's a period piece within. Routhland (opposite, bottom) is an 1817, low-roofedvariant of the French Colonial style made classic by the gable and gallery.

NATCHEZ - 1818

Originally in the Federal style, Monmouth became a Greek Revival mansion in the mid-1800s when owned by General John A. Quitman, Mexican War hero, Mississippi governor and congressman. When recently restored, it was furnished in the ornate style the Quitmans are thought to have favored. The towering ceiling and doorways of the central hall are typical of Natchez' early era. The doors are faux bois. The front and back of the house are across the page. For extra living space, the new owners enclosed the rear galleries at both ends, then clad the new exterior walls with fixed shutters. In the past, real shutters might have been used for sun protection.

NATCHEZ - 1796

Gloucester was much smaller than this when built. The portico and three bays at left (a bay is a window or door opening) were added in 1815. Thus a rather plain, severe house became a magnificent mansion. The angled ends of the house necessitated hip roofs, which tend to soften the lines of the dwelling.

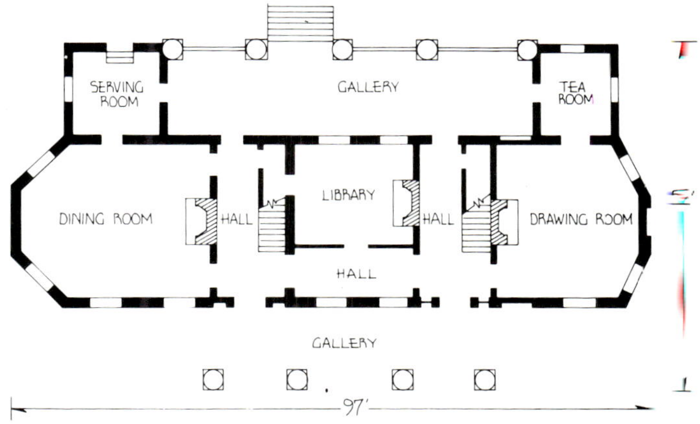

NATCHEZ

Hope Farm (left, top) is two houses joined by galleries. The front section, shown here, dates from 1789 when Natchez was governed by the Spanish. The larger rear section, with two floors and double galleries, was built in 1744 when the English ruled. Hawthorne (left, bottom) was built in 1814. Of Federal design, with a lovely fanlight spanning the door and sidelights, it is quite simple but nowhere nearly as simple and severe as Hope Farm.

NATCHEZ - 1782

There are some who maintain that the Elms is definitely Spanish Colonial because of its thick walls, low ceilings, courtyards and other features. But this feeling stems in part from wishful imagining. When built, the house was much smaller and probably of vernacular style. (A drawing done in 1857 shows it very definitely of vernacular style.) It is, nonetheless, an intriguing, delightful home with a great variety of eclectic features.

NATCHEZ - 1784

Richmond is three buildings in one. The first was a French Colonial raised cottage (opposite page, bottom)—a story-and-a-half frame structure atop a brick basement. It had galleries on the south (front) and north sides. Then in 1832, a new owner added the incomparable Greek Revival wing (above). It, too, had a raised brick basement finished with stucco. The main body of the wing was sided with bevel-edged boards. A balustrade above the cornice partially hid the gabled roof, which had parapets at the ends. The double parlors (right), with Ionic pilasters and elegant moldings, are in this part of the house. Finally, in 1860, a very simple two-story brick bedroom wing was added to the other end of the house.

NATCHEZ

At the junction of Washington Street and Wall, fine old houses stand on each of the four corners. Dixie (above) is one of them. The others are the Griffith-McComas house, Holly Hedges and Texada. Dixie is a very simple Greek Revival house in comparison with the west wing of Richmond. But in its simplicity it has a comfortable charm. Note the connected chimneys—a characteristic of the Greek Revival style.

NATCHEZ

The Briars (this page) was built in 1814. It is a very sophisticated home despite the simplicity of its plan and shape. The fanlighted doorways and the dormers are particularly lovely. The size of the round-headed dormer windows, coupled with the fact that there are square-headed dormers in back, assure that the upper floor is bright and airy. The house originally had only a front (east) gallery. A rear gallery (actually a double gallery, because the ground slopes away from the house) was added at some time, but the job was done so well that this is hardly apparent.

On the facing page at the top is Glenburnie, a home of two eras. The wing at right was built in 1833. It is an example of the Federal style. The gabled and pedimented Georgian Revival section dates from 1901. Oakland (opposite, bottom) is a refined brick house with one not-so-modest feature: mahogany window sash. Built in 1835, it looks small but has big rooms and sixteen-foot ceilings. A brick outbuilding is behind it.

NATCHEZ

Elgin (above) is typical of Valley plantation homes that were built more to beat the climate than to make a show. It is one-room deep and has wide galleries to shade the many large doors and windows opening onto them. The first part of the house was built around 1800, and it was enlarged and remodeled several times after that. Melrose (opposite) is one of the classics of the Greek Revival style. Built in 1845, it is impeccable and austere—as befits a classic. No major changes have ever been made in it. The detached kitchen behind the house is still in use. Floor plans are at right.

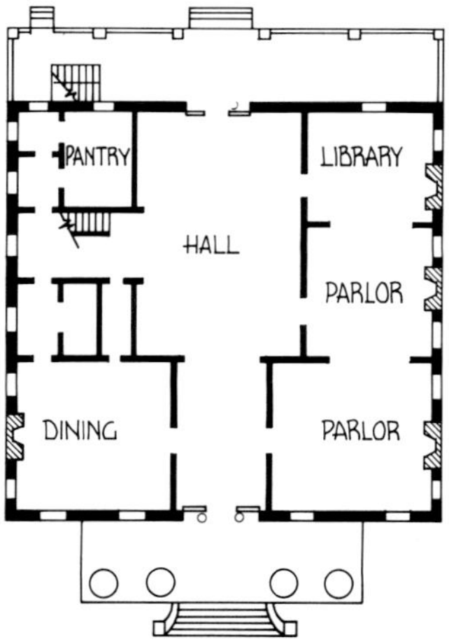

PLAN A

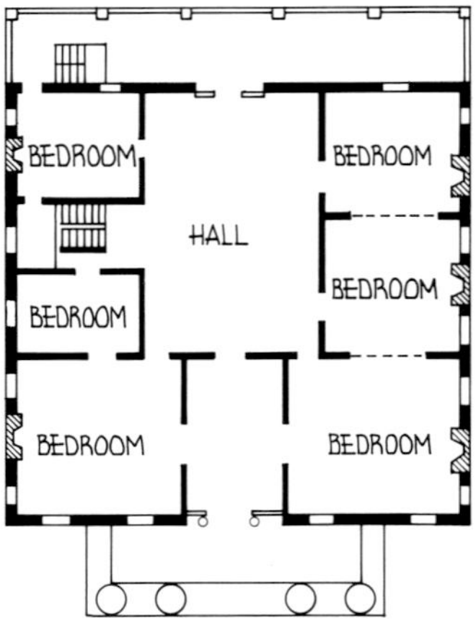

PLAN B

NATCHEZ

Winchester (opposite, top) and Williamsburg (below) were built at roughly the same time in the early 1800s. They almost face each other across the street and look much alike until you examine them closely.

NATCHEZ

The house above is of a later era. Its style is less easily classified than that of the houses opposite. Call it just a comfortable place with double front porches. It is perfectly maintained and has an exceptional garden.

NATCHEZ

Edgewood (left) is dated from the 1850s. It is a fascinating and charming combination of Corinthian columns and Victorian brackets. And it is made the more interesting by the gable, which serves no purpose except to frame the gently arched French doors. The Towers (below) is even more fanciful. The doorways are classic but nothing else is. The house was built in 1827, remodeled in 1860.

NATCHEZ - 1836

When Elms Court was built, it was similar to other Greek Revival dwellings in Natchez. It had flush siding and a portico as well as its present doorway, which is framed by Ionic columns supporting an entablature with transom light above. But in 1852 new owners transformed the house into a romantic villa. They replaced the portico with double galleries and added two symmetrical one-story wings with galleries. Then they "curtained" the entire facade with ironwork such as Natchez had never known. Finally, they painted the front wall to simulate ashlar masonry in varying hues of brown. (This may have been beautiful, but happily the wall is once again white.)

At the same time, the original interior, with four rooms on the main floor, was altered somewhat. Changes included enlarging the dining room by enclosing the old rear gallery (which also incorporated a small sitting room). Two early mantels were replaced with Gothic designs. However, much of the trim was left intact.

NATCHEZ

Glen Auburn (above) was built in 1830, remodeled forty years later. It is an imposing Victorian on a terraced hillside in downtown Natchez. Its vivid coloration is more typical of New Orleans than Natchez, but it is by no means unique. Several Natchez houses are even more strongly colored and a good number are in soft pastel shades. The J.C. Wilkins house (left, top), built in 1827, is now the Chamber of Commerce office. The dentiled frieze, the doorway with its bullseye-lighted transom, the curving steps—everything about the place is perfect. The roofline of the Griffith-McComas house (left) makes it appear to flow down the hill on which it stands. A 1793, one-room-deep, downtown structure of vernacular design, it has great appeal which the present owners have enhanced in their do-it-yourself restoration. The original lower rear gallery was enclosed some years ago to make a kitchen. The outside stair still provides the only access to the second floor.

NATCHEZ - 1800. There is more about Linden on the following pages.

LINDEN

Linden is prime evidence that a vernacular house (with Federal leanings) can be gorgeous. The facade with its 98-foot gallery, slender columns, second-story balustrade, two-tiered portico and splendid doorway is beautiful. The big galleried wings (one with fixed louvers to give shade) added in the rear blend with the original house. And though the detailing is simple, the interiors are lovely. The fireplaces are among the best in the Lower Mississippi Valley. The punkah that fanned diners is incomparable.

INFORMATION
CENTER

NATCHEZ - 1795

From its commanding position, Connelly's Tavern looks out toward the Mississippi. It is a unique building that served as both a home and tavern. French Colonial (some say Spanish Colonial) in style, it draws attention from afar partly because of its prominent position and partly because of the long, delicate-looking galleries. Then one notices the roof, which is both hipped and gabled. Where the gabled portion stops, the front and rear slopes break slightly upward. This is known as a canted roof and it was used on many of the Valley's galleried homes.

The upper-story living quarters of the Tavern were, understandably, detailed more carefully than the floor below. Many of the ceilings are arched. In back (below) is a moat with bridges across it to the three doors.

NATCHEZ - 1853

Lansdowne is so well proportioned that it looks small even though it measures 60 by 68 feet. It is an outstanding Greek Revival house raised five feet above ground and reached by gracefully flared steps. The portico is of classical design and proportions; the gallery stretching across the entire rear of the house is considerably simpler. The brick walls are plastered.

The interior, with a fourteen-foot-wide central hall separating the parlor, dining room and butler's pantry on one side from three bedrooms on the other, is no less beautiful. The parlor is shown opposite. Architecturally, the treatment is essentially academic. Fancy plaster work is limited to centerpieces and cornices (which are not fancy). But the decorative treatment is Rococo. It has been said that Lansdowne is "one of the most complete statements of the Rococo Revival taste in America to survive from the mid-Nineteenth Century". "Survive" is the key word, because the house is still in the same family and they have meticulously preserved everything about it. Modern amenities—bathrooms, a kitchen (the original was in one of the two two-story, four-room outbuildings), electricity—have been kept to a minimum.

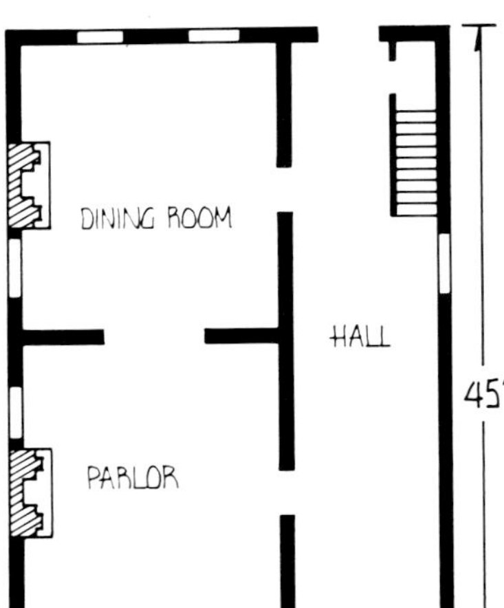
DINING ROOM
HALL
45′
PARLOR
33′

SPEED LIMIT 25

NATCHEZ

These three town houses are all of Greek Revival design. The Banker's house, 1835, at the top of the facing page is obviously the largest. It has at the right end a galleried wing that is almost impossible to show because of the magnolias. The portico with its fine frieze adds much to the formality of the place. The Van Court house (opposite, bottom) is a typical side-hall residence and was built at about the same time. The original brick facing has been stuccoed. While the ornamental iron portico relieves the severity of the facade, it tends to detract from the handsome fanlighted doorway. The Dr. Dubs house on this page is in form a northern Greek Revival house and has a plan like the Van Court's. Seen from the side (above) it is larger than you might first guess. The small wing to the right of the front door is properly proportioned to the main body (too often wings are more prominent than they should be). This is also true of the two-story rear wing. The brickwork is very skillfully crafted.

NATCHEZ

The William Ailes house (left) is a Greek Revival dwelling typical of antebellum Natchez homes built by the working middle class. The dormers (above) have unusual, beveled glazed corners.

Much remodeled Holly Hedges (right) presents a gracious, friendly face to the public. The arched dormer windows are beautiful (compare them with those on page 38), as are the interiors. But the house as a whole is very simple. The rear roof line is awkward as a result of an 1832 remodeling.

The Lisle-Shields house (left, bottom) is a splendidly executed late Greek Revival residence built shortly before the War between the States.

The center part of Wigwam (right, bottom) was built in 1790. Wings and eclectic features were added sometime later.

NATCHEZ

The Burn (opposite, top) is the first documented Greek Revival house in Natchez. It dates from 1834. The dominating portico has Doric columns and entablature. The pilasters with applied vertical moldings more or less repeat the lines of the triglyphs on the frieze. Cottage Gardens (opposite, bottom left) looks very similar until you analyze it. It is more Federal than Greek.

The derelict mansion (opposite, bottom right) is one of those sad stories that the relentless Mississippi has to tell. It is Weymouth Hall, built in 1820 and remodeled thirty years later. The only Greek Revival house in Natchez with a fully raised basement (what appears to be the first floor is the basement), it stands on the bluff high above the river; and the bluff is being washed away. Weymouth Hall may soon be in the river.

The railed structure above the peak of Weymouth Hall's roof would, in the North, be called a widow's or captain's walk. Some southerners call it a belvedere, although belvederes are generally thought to be gazebo-like enclosed structures similar to that on Houmas house, page 119. Whatever the name, the space could be used for viewing the surrounding countryside or, in this case, for keeping watch on the river traffic; but whether it actually was we don't know. The chances are that its main purpose was decorative; and in some houses, as here, it was used as a lantern to bring light and air into the attic space and perhaps the floor below (note the glassed area directly below the deck).

CHURCH HILL - 1828

Oak Grove was constructed in two sections, the last work being done in 1853. It is a distinctive house with galleries across the back as well as the front (those in back have been partially enclosed). Note the doorway with pretty little stairs on the annex at right.

FAYETTE - 1790

The great houses of Natchez are not confined within the city limits. Nearby to the north and south there are many others; and while these are generally much simpler (partly because they were or are on working plantations), they are nevertheless interesting and beautiful. Springfield, like nearby Oak Grove on the preceding page, is one of these. Built by a Virginian, it is said to be the first great house in the Natchez area to have double galleries stretching across the entire facade.

WOODVILLE - 1832

Hampton Hall combines the Greek Revival and Federal styles as a good many of the early-Nineteenth Century Mississippi houses did. Because of its height and its perch at the top of a rise, it has an unfortunate boxy appearance but the double-galleried portico more than compensates for this. The doorways are beautiful and matching except for the fact that the first-floor fanlight has a shorter radius and is therefore higher. The house has a staircase that rises in an ellipse to the top floor under the gable roof.

WOODVILLE

Because the highway north to Natchez loops around Woodville, it's easy to miss the many fine homes in this little old community. The Carnot-Posey home (opposite, top) is one of these. It was built in 1845. The brick-floored gallery and circular columns are a recent change. The earlier gallery had a raised wood floor and square columns.

The Argue house (opposite, bottom) dates from the Nineteenth Century and has suffered to some extent from the ravages of time. It is of vernacular Federal design. Built into a hillside, it is two stories tall in back.

WOODVILLE - 1809

In 1876 Dr. L.W. Magruder decided he had been plagued by the sun long enough. There was just no way that he could sit happily on his lower gallery when the sun was in the southern sky. So he had a canopy built around it. And since he was in the building mood and the house (above) needed work, he had the carpenters spruce up the whole place. That, of course, was in Victorian days, so it wasn't surprising that the doctor and carpenters built more or less in that style. And it is rather too bad that they did, because the sunshade does not help the house visually, and the other Victorian touches had a slightly detrimental effect, too. Because, if you were to strip these additions from the house, you would find it to be a charming vernacular design typical of its early days. Still, you can't blame the doctor for what he did—or, more properly, permitted. As ill-conceived as it was, the canopy was needed: a south-facing, unprotected gallery in the Lower Valley is a misery nine months of the year. And as for the other Victorian touches, well, it has always been natural for people to remodel in the current mode. (Restoring a house to its original style was rarely, if ever, thought of in the 1800s.)

WOODVILLE - 1832

The Lewis house is so imposing that, viewing it only from the front, you have no idea it is only one room deep; and even though it has, over the years, been added to, it is still only one room deep so that air can circulate through it and keep it cool in summer.

PORT GIBSON - 1851

To the average northerner, the Lewis house opposite is the typical Mississippi Valley house. But the Gage house here is the true Valley house (if you can say there is such a thing). It has a light, airy, cool look beckoning you inside to escape the heat.

PORT GIBSON VICINITY - 1860

Windsor took two years and $175,000 to build. It had a raised basement and two floors, each with six rooms. To one end was attached a two-story, galleried service wing. It survived the War between the States, then burned to the ground in 1890 when a guest dropped a lighted cigar or match into a wastebasket. All that is left are the twenty-two Corinthian columns, which rose from piers level with the first-floor galleries, and remnants of the upper-story iron balustrade.

PORT GIBSON - 1850

Oak Square, the largest house in Port Gibson, is a vernacular home given Greek Revival overtones by the twenty-two-foot Corinthian columns on the gallery. The doorway is unique—with wide double doors, extraordinarily wide sidelights, and a transom window over all. Sidelights and transom are leaded. The stairway, also unique, rises from the middle of the great hall, doubles back on both sides at a landing. Above the landing (but below the second floor), behind a balustrade is a sizable, brightly lighted cross hall reached by the back stairs.

PORT GIBSON - 1820

The Greek Revival style was far from being cut-and-dried, bound by rigid rules, as the McDougall house (right) shows. The columns at the ends of the porch are square and mainly smooth (despite the applied moldings); the two in the middle are circular and fluted. The latter are Corinthian, though the capitals are much modified versions of true Corinthian capitals, which are ornamented with closely clustered acanthus leaves. The entablature is also suggestive of that used in the Corinthian order.

The dormers are like many in New Orleans. The windows are rectangular but topped by an arched molding applied to the gables. Pilasters are applied to the corners of the gables.

PORT GIBSON - 1830

The Judge Coleman house (opposite, top) is a simple, low clapboarded place. Note that the louvered shutters to the right of the double door are open while the others are closed. Many Valley home owners still follow the old practice of shuttering their windows—and sometimes doors—at night. But the main purpose of shutters is to screen out the hot sun; and to that end they are always hung outside to keep the sun off the glass.

PORT GIBSON - 1833

Idlewild (above) is a serenely formal raised cottage of Greek Revival design. It has the horizontal flush board siding that is supposed to typify Revival houses not made of masonry. The wood balustrade on the gallery is of moderately elaborate design.

PORT GIBSON

The Disharoon house (opposite, top) is another charming two-story residence with double galleries and slender columns. Originally it also had double galleries in the rear. It does not appear to be the kind of house that would have the spiral staircase pictured above, but Valley people evidently liked spiral stairs. Disharoon was built in 1830. At the bottom of the opposite page is the Spencer house (1840) with sturdy square columns. I somehow doubt that practicalities entered the old-timers' heads when they chose between square and circular columns, but the former are easily rebuilt when they rot out. Replacing round columns is expensive, sometimes difficult.

VICKSBURG

Vicksburg is a city of very steep hills; consequently the old houses, like these, are often perched high above the streets. Anchuca (above) was built in 1830. Initially it was a one-story wood structure. About ten years later the owner added a second story and a "pretentious front". Because this faces north, there was no need to shield the first-floor windows from the sun. On the other hand, Cedar Grove (opposite) looks west over the river, so the second-story gallery helps to shade the lower windows (but not as sundown approaches). In the back of the house there are also double galleries. The first-floor gallery is level with the ground; the upper is reached by a handsome flight of straight stairs built of ornamental iron and extending out into the garden (instead of leading from the lower level to the upper, as was usual).

VICKSBURG

McRaven (opposite) started life as a frontier cottage with a brick floor and plaster made of marble dust, sugar, molasses and horsehair and stained with blueberry dye. In 1836 the middle section in a regionalized Greek Revival style was added. Finally, in 1849, the front section, the only part visible in the photograph, was built. It is a mixture of Greek Revival and Italianate.

Floweree (above) dates from 1877 and is pure Victorian. The almost overpowering portico with its square brick columns replaced a portico with clusters of slender wood columns.

Planter's Hall (right) housed a bank on the first floor when it was built in 1834. The bank president lived on the second floor. Except for the facade, it is a rather forbidding building. The treatment of the two doors contrasts in an interesting and attractive way.

VICKSBURG

The two houses above plus the one almost hidden behind it but shown in the black-and-white photo represent one of Vicksburg's newest and biggest restoration projects. Walking up Crawford Street, you pass first the Mitchell house (1878), then the Lane House (1824) and finally come to the Upton Young house (1873). The first two are rather standard, galleried Mississippi Valley town houses; the last is Italianate. The doorways are especially interesting for the manner in which they are tied together. It was obviously intended that a balcony should be outside the upper door but there apparently never was one.

VICKSBURG - 1791

The Seargent S. Prentiss house (right) is, in spite of the wires that mar it, a charmer in its simplicity. It is now used for offices. The second-floor gallery extends over the sidewalk as in New Orleans. The lower floor had plastered brick walls. The second-story walls were of half-timber construction with brick fill between timbers. They're now clapboarded.

VICKSBURG - 1873

The Corners was a wedding present from father to daughter. The Victorian porch conceals the fact that the brick house is quite severe—a vernacular Greek Revival structure. The doorway, flanked by five windows extending to the floor, is typically Greek Revival. The cornice and frieze on the wing added to the side of the house are also classic. But the windows in the wing and the adjacent house wall have Victorian pediments. It is an interesting but pleasant mixture. Note that the wing is connected to the main body of the house only by a sort of suspended tunnel.

VICKSBURG

If you came upon these houses in New England, you would not give them a second thought because they would seem to belong. But they look out of place in the Mississippi Valley, and you can't help wondering how they happened to be built.

Plain Gables (left) was built around 1830. Except for the doorway and two end chimneys, it is much like the Cape Cod house of the 1840s. Certainly there are many houses like it in various parts of the United States.

The two-story McNutt house was begun in 1826, enlarged by Governor Alexander McNutt in 1830, altered again in the 1850s and once again in the present century. It needs a steeper roof and central chimney to pass for a true New England Colonial.

REDWOOD - 1840

Blakely sits high on a hill with its rear gallery (not shown; to the left in the picture above) overlooking the vast Valley. Although the Blake family has occupied it almost from the start, the house is only half finished. The original steep-roofed, one-story log house was built and occupied by highwaymen in the early 1800s. In 1840, shortly after Colonel Benson Blake took it over, he erected the large two-story vernacular addition. He told his wife that a duplicate addition would replace the cabin, but he was never able to keep his promise. As a result, although the house is grandly beautiful as you drive up toward the end pictured, it looks odd when viewed head on (right). Still, it has compelling appeal.

VICKSBURG

The Nineteenth Century house above is next door to the Prentiss house (Page 77) and makes an interesting contrast to it. Whereas the latter is of extremely simple design, this one has a highly stylized facade. Note particularly the sunburst pediments above the downstairs windows and door.

The William Lake house (right, top) was built in 1835. It is a vernacular version of the Greek Revival style. One could wish that the gable window was fan-shaped. But the doorway is magnificent—almost an exact duplicate of the doorways on the more famous 1835 house known as Pemberton's Headquarters. The door and sidelights are recessed a couple of feet behind the Ionic columns, which along with the adjacent pilasters support the entablature.

The very Greek Revival house (bottom) was built in 1859. It has just been restored. Note that the front windows extend to the floor but are not jib windows. Despite the practicality of jibs, they were not widely used in the Mississippi Valley probably because they're best suited to houses with exceptionally high ceilings. This house has high ceilings but they are not exceptional.

JACKSON

Manship is a marvelous Gothic Revival house of arches and elaborate ornamentation. Built in 1857, it was probably inspired by a design in a pattern book written by Andrew Jackson Downing. The front of the house is at right; the side, in the large picture. The State of Mississippi, which bought and restored the place in 1975, says the house is painted its original olive drab (with cream trim, bright green shutters, grayish-pink chimneys). It is a sorry description of such an unusual color. Inside are a parlor, sitting room, dining room, three bedrooms and bathing room.

Below is the Boyd house (1856), a one-story Greek Revival. The hoops between columns are a gentle touch seen in several Valley homes.

NORTH CARROLLTON and GRENADA

Cotesworth, in North Carrollton, has a modern look although it was built in 1840 and enlarged a few years later. Of Greek Revival design, it is much simpler than most of the Greek Revival homes in Natchez and Louisiana. (In a very general way, this is characteristic of houses in northern Mississippi.) But the real architectural gem on the plantation is the small law library (opposite) built by the owner a few hundred feet away so he could escape disturbance. It is a simple hexagon ornamented by the elegant cupola and fancy portico.

Evergreen, dating from the middle 1800s in Grenada, was built of brick rather than the wood normally used in the area and made use of prefabricated decorative building materials. (Woodwork, etc., made in mills came into use in the Lower Mississippi Valley shortly before the War between the States. Previously it had been handcrafted by slaves and itinerant craftsmen.) At the time I saw the house it had been torn apart and was being rebuilt. The only thing pictureable was the windows (left) with their hat-like architraves.

YAZOO CITY

The large double-galleried house and its numerous dependencies opposite form an island in a vast expanse of delta land. The Nineteenth Century structure is handsome but unimportant here. It simply illustrates why many plantation houses grew so big. Being isolated in the country and served only by dirt roads or boats, they were meant to house as well as feed guests invited to dinners, balls, etc. Families in those days were also very large.

CARROLLTON

One of the interesting things about Mississippi Valley houses is that you cannot always tell whether a home has been remodeled. In some cases even the owners don't know. The house below is an example. The house proper is quite severe but the elaborate treatment of the double galleries hides the fact. Question: Was the house built this way or were the galleries added at a later date—as the break in the roofline indicates they may have been?

HOLLY SPRINGS - 1840

Sandusky (below) is probably the most appealing house in the only Valley town that comes close in matching the number of marvelous old houses found in Natchez. It stands on a corner and is H-shaped. A modest but classic gallery extends across almost the entire front, at left. The cross-arm, facing the side street, also has a gallery but the roof is lower to give more shade. Architecturally the house is fairly formal, but the general air is of quiet informality.

HOLLY SPRINGS

Holly Springs is younger than the communities farther south; consequently its old homes date back to only about 1830. Because of this, they are to large degree in the Greek Revival architectural style and to a somewhat lesser degree in the Victorian style. They form an important and lovely collection.

As a very general rule, the houses are only one story high, so although they are of fairly modest size, they cover considerable area (but are rarely long and thin as many are in Natchez). Roughly half the houses are raised but seldom more than a few feet.

Shown here is Crump Place (opposite, top), built in 1836. The facade is clad with horizontal flush boards; the rest of the house, with clapboards. The front steps are recessed into the portico instead of extending out from it. Above is Tuckahoe—a free spirit—with an odd but attractive Palladian-style front on the porch. The dining room and kitchen are in the raised basement. The Greek Revival interiors are from Walter Place. Arches and domes (actually a half dome in the stairwell) are a characteristic of the Greek Revival style; but the octagonal towers with battlements that flank the classic portico (small picture far left) most certainly are not. They just satisfied the builder's desire to be different.

HOLLY SPRINGS

Both of the houses on the facing page are Greek Revival in style, although Featherston (bottom) has a Federal doorway. But Whittens (this page) is a conservative Victorian. It was built in 1840, five years before Cochran Place (opposite, top). This simply confirms the fact that the two styles overlapped in the 1840-1860 period.

HOLLY SPRINGS

Hamilton Place (opposite, top), Latoka (opposite, bottom) and Linden Terrace (this page) were built between 1838 and 1844. All are brick; all are essentially Greek Revival in style; but Hamilton Place looks more like a southern house than the others.

The rectangular recesses in Linden Terrace's brick frieze were probably meant to be filled with plaques or sculptures of some sort. The difference between the front and side-street doorways is interesting. Unless you were told beforehand which was the front door, you would not know which you should knock on.

A comparison of Linden Terrace with Hamilton Place shows how a long columned gallery relieves the severity of a facade.

HOLLY SPRINGS

The 1839 builder of Mosswood (above) relieved the straight lines of the vernacular Greek Revival style with arched lights in the door and a fanlight over the gable window. The Magnolias (right and below) is also a Greek Revival house, but here the entire doorway is arched like the lacy iron grillwork on the porch and the window above it is of Gothic design with diamond-shaped panes.

Oakleigh (opposite, top) has a monumental classic portico with a small balcony outside the second-story doorway. The cornice alternates dentils and pendants. The window overtreatment is Victorian. The Victorian look of Grey Gables (bottom pictures, opposite) was added: Originally the house was a simple cottage. Interiors of both of these homes are on the next two pages.

HOLLY SPRINGS

The detailing throughout Oakleigh is elaborate and gorgeous. The double parlors, which can be cut off from one another by recessed sliding doors, are above; the lovely stair hall is at right; the dining room, with rounded end and *faux marbre* baseboards, is at far right, bottom.

Grey Gables (other three pictures) is equally beautiful in a slightly simpler vein. The trim, featured by semi-dark rope moldings against a light background, is very unusual and effective. The stairway has a more delicate feeling than that in Oakleigh because the rail is supported by only a single baluster on each tread, but the almost free-standing newel post is massive. In both houses the plaster ceiling centerpieces are magnificent.

Louisiana

1. Alexandria
2. Baton Rouge
3. Bermuda
4. Burnside
5. Clinton
6. Convent
7. Darrow
8. Donaldsonville
9. Edgard
10. Franklin
11. French Settlement
12. Geismar
13. Hahnville
14. Harahan
15. Jackson
16. Mandeville
17. Mansura
18. Nachitoches
19. Napoleonville
20. Natchez
21. New Iberia
22. New Orleans
23. New Roads
24. Reserve
25. St. Francisville
26. St. Martinville
27. Springfield
28. Sunset
29. Thibodeaux
30. Vacherie
31. Wallace
32. Washington
33. White Castle

NEW ORLEANS - 1788

Madame John's Legacy is a duplicate of the original house, which was built in 1726. It is one of New Orleans' premier examples of the early French Colonial architectural style. The raised basement was first used for storage but is now an exhibition gallery operated by the Louisiana State Museum, which owns the property. A double gallery in the rear faces a courtyard and galleried one-room-deep garconniere. Also in the rear, separate from the house, is the kitchen. The house is not so crude as it appears. The slightly arched, inswinging casement windows have a surprising delicacy. The plainness of the woodwork is relieved by simple moldings, panels and iron hardware.

NEW ORLEANS - 1831

Despite the second-story balcony with its simple but delicate iron balustrade, the Hermann-Grima house seems out of place in the increasingly sleazy French Quarter. For one thing, it has been beautifully restored and many houses have not been. More important, it is more formal looking than the majority of houses in the Quarter. This formality has been achieved by a nice blending of Georgian, Greek Revival and French Colonial features. Two wood-balustraded balconies overlook the large courtyard behind the house. At left is the central hall and stairway, with brass newel post. Many interior doors have transoms.

NEW ORLEANS

In New Orleans' early days the houses were fairly low, as at right. But in the 1800s, as the French Quarter became crowded and Anglo-American influences became stronger, they began to shoot up. Few, however, went over three stories. The one above has four. Because of its high ceilings, it is the equivalent of a modern five or six-story building. The monumental side doorway is reached by stairs enclosed behind the iron grilles at street level.

Houses at the north and east sides of the Quarter tend to be smaller. The two here are Creole cottages. Three things characterize this type of house: They were low to the ground, flush with the sidewalk. They had steep gable roofs sloping front to back. The roofs overhung the sidewalk. At first the overhang was attached to the facade and often supported by horizontal iron bearers. Later it was incorporated into the roof as here. Most cottages had four openings (bays) in front. Some had two or three.

NEW ORLEANS

The LeCarpentier or Beauregard home (above) was built in 1827. It's a raised columned and pilastered Greek Revival house with French doors on either side of the entrance. The ceiling centerpiece is elaborate yet fairly restrained by contrast to some in other Valley homes.

The main body of the Gauche house (opposite), 1856, is very stiff despite the cornice treatment and very ornate balustrade on the balconies; but the extensive L-shaped rear wing (top picture) looks more at home in the deep South.

The small picture shows one of the carriageways that separate many French Quarter houses and sometimes run right through houses.

NEW ORLEANS - 1800

There are not many plantation houses left in New Orleans from early times, but the Pitot house, facing Bayou St. John, is in excellent repair and worth a visit some Thursday, when it is opened to the public by the Louisiana Landmark Society. Recently restored by the Society, it's a prize example of the early French Colonial style—a raised house with a great hip roof, wide galleries, large ground-floor columns and slender colonettes above, shuttered French doors, slightly arched casements (as in Madame John's Legacy), an outside stair to the upper rear gallery (opposite), a one-room-deep plan with cabinets at the ends of the rear galleries.

NEW ORLEANS

Left: The box mantel and boxed-in chimney in the parlor of the Pitot house are typical of the early 1800s though handsomer than most. The parlor is on the second floor and is sandwiched between large bedrooms. Below are three other nearby houses on Bayou St. John. At top is the Old Spanish Custom House, which was originally a home. It dates from 1784. Next is the Blanc house, built in 1834 along more classic lines. At bottom is the doorway of a similar semi-classical house of the same era.

NEW ORLEANS

These houses in the Garden District display the Orleanians' fascination with the ornamentation of their homes' exteriors. This was not always limited to the facades: The huge Robinson house (right, top), built in 1865, and the Morris house below it (1869) were also treated on the sides. Ironwork was the favorite material used but wood was frequently handled in much the same way (as at left). And although many home owners eschewed such lacework, they still achieved a highly ornamental effect through careful, beautiful detailing (as directly below).

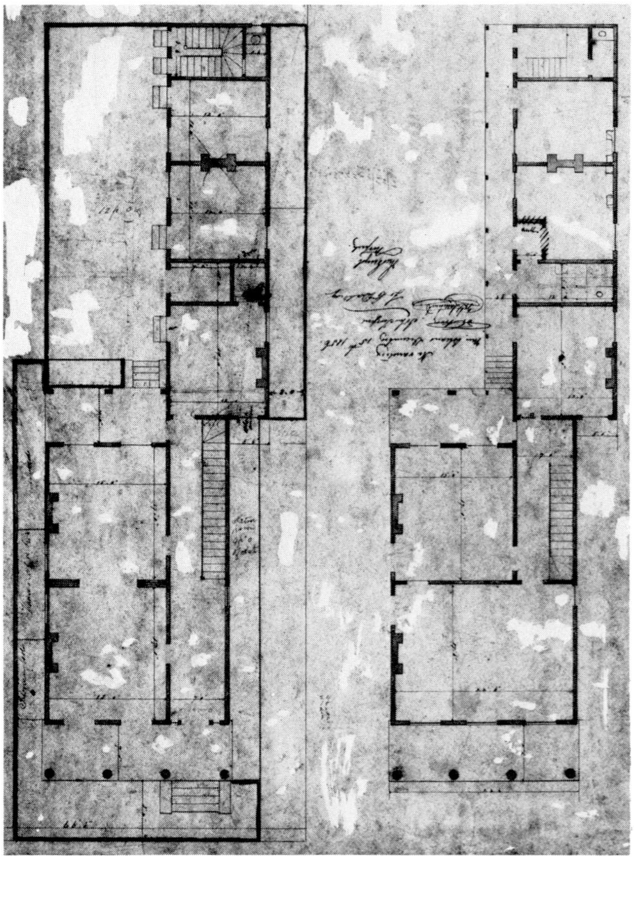

NEW ORLEANS

The ancient plan of the Dabney house is confusing. (1) It is lettered upside down. The bottom of the plan as you see it is the front of the house. (2) There is no explanation of what the heavy lines around the first-floor plan, left, stand for. (3) The house has been changed since the plan was drawn. Nevertheless, the plan gives an idea of how New Orleans houses were frequently laid out. They were not very wide but stretched back and back. A courtyard or garden was generally hidden from the street in the angle of the L.

NEW ORLEANS

Both of the Greek Revival houses on these two pages were built in the middle 1800s. The Dabney house (opposite) was given Ionic columns on the first floor; Corinthian on the second. The use of ironwork was restrained. The tall paneled interior doors were crowned by projecting cornices. The columns on the entrance porch of the Robert A. Grinnan house on this page belong to the Composite order, which was similar to the Corinthian but had Ionic volutes as a feature of the capitals. The same capitals are used on the square columns indoors. Note the elaborate over-door treatments outdoors and in; the splendid wall cornices and friezes.

NEW ORLEANS

Wealthy Orleanians obviously did not spend all their money on the embellishment of their homes' exteriors. As the Brevard house indicates, the interiors were given the same treatment. Incredible chandeliers hanging from equally incredible centerpieces; graceful arches (in this case the arch helps to divide the huge drawing room into two somewhat more intimate areas and at the same time takes the curse off a long stretch of blank ceiling); marble fireplaces; carved over-door treatments; heavy, handsome cornices and friezes—these were just some of the interior architectural features. And they were augmented, of course, by equally beautiful wallcoverings, draperies and furnishings, a great many of which were imported from Europe.

NEW ORLEANS

New Orleans has hundreds of houses that are built close to the ground, but the early practice of raising houses persisted far into the Nineteench Century, as shown here. In fact, the practice is still observed to some extent. The main reasons for raising houses were to get them above flood level and to put an air layer between the damp earth and living quarters. But the aesthetic effect was substantial, too. An elevated entrance is dramatic (as well as formal). It pulls the eye upward to encompass the whole house. But whether it is more welcoming is moot. Certainly the handicapped would not think it so.

NEW ORLEANS

The entrances—front doors and space around them—designed by the old architects and builders put modern versions to shame. They were not only more attractive and more inviting; they actually were better proportioned for the passage of people and furniture through them. You would expect such an entrance to the huge Aldrich-Genella house (directly above). But in the Garden District, even very simple houses such as that at bottom right have handsome entrances.

NEW ORLEANS

On this page, a pair of lovely homes in the French Colonial style. The main entrance to the house at top is on the second floor—reached by a pair of steps that curve up to it from opposite directions. Below the landing, concealed from the camera by the mass of evergreens, is a ground-floor door. Because it's on a city lot, the lower house lacks galleries on the sides; otherwise it is almost exactly like the typical Louisiana plantation house.

On the facing page, a pair of Greek Revival homes in the subtle colors that make the Garden District so inviting. The house at bottom might lead you to believe you are walking down a New England street. The upper section of the high garden wall at the left of the house is louvered to let breezes into the garden yet assure privacy.

1037

NEW ORLEANS

Shotgun houses are found in many cities but under other names. They are so-called because theoretically you could fire a gun the length of the long, thin house without hitting anything. They originated in New Orleans about 1840; have two, three or even four bays; and usually have hip roofs. The one above, with five chimneys—one per room—, is prettier than most. That opposite is a charmer because of its marvelous gingerbread and color scheme. It is ivory—almost yellow—with pale green trim and lemon accents. The two-story addition at the rear of the shotgun at right makes the house a form of camelback. Camelbacking began when one-story Creole cottages were united with the separate two-story kitchens behind them.

SPRINGFIELD - 1820

The Carter plantation house, once called Sycamore (opposite), is modest in scale and design and for that very reason something of a relief from the enormous, pretentious plantation houses not far away. It is on low, undistinguished land and must originally have seemed like nothing more than an unusually pretty farm house. But the present owners have partially ringed it around with irregular man-made stock ponds with water spouts that greatly beautify the setting.

BURNSIDE - 1840

Houmas (this page) is a glorious modified Greek Revival plantation house surmounted by a belvedere that afforded a sweeping view of the surrounding country and nearby river. The stringer of the winding stair is decorated with applied scrolls—a common practice in the Lower Mississippi Valley's homes and throughout the country in that era.

GEISMAR - 1841

You pull on a bell at a rickety gate and an old man comes scurrying from somewhere. He is the only person living at the plantation called Ashland or Belle Helene and he talks mainly about the many movies that were made in the huge house. The Hollywood people, he says, wrecked the place. Whether this be true, the destruction or collapse of the interior is all too evident. Only a few centerpieces and moldings are intact. But from a distance the magnificence is inescapable. The enormous square columns completely surrounding the mansion are dominant. The upper gallery is subordinate because it is behind the columns and attached to them only by projecting joists.

DARROW - 1812

The Hermitage (left) speaks for itself. Although completely surrounded by Doric columns rising from the ground to the roof, the huge hip roof and general plan are French Colonial.

BURNSIDE - 1855

Tezcuco is a one-and-a-half-story raised French Colonial done in the Greek Revival manner. It has wrought-iron balustrades on the front and side galleries. The builder was a connection of the Bringier family, which also built Hermitage, Bocage and White Hall. The last was destroyed by fire followed by vandals.

BURNSIDE - 1801

The Bocage you see today is not the Bocage that was built as a wedding present. It was extensively remodeled in 1841, presumably by James H. Dakin, one of the South's early great architects. He enlarged the entablature and added a high parapet that completely conceals the roof, which is shaped like a W. But the oddest thing about the Greek Revival structure is the square columns. Starting from either side there is a large column, a wide space, a large column, a wide space, a large column, then a narrower space and a small column. The space between the two small columns equals the wide spaces between large columns and it used to be filled with a flight of stairs to the entrance on the upper gallery. Note, too, that the second story is considerably taller than the first.

SAN FRANCISCO. More on the next page

EAST BANK RIVER ROAD, NEAR NEW ORLEANS

The incredibly ornate house here and on the preceding page was first called St. Frusquin, a name from a French slang term meaning "one's all". It's easy to believe that Edmond Bozonier Marmillion, who built the place in 1856, spent his all on it. Today St. Frusquin has been corrupted to San Francisco. There is no house like it anywhere: enormous and flamboyant; French Colonial overlaid with Gothic features. It is in Reserve.

D'Estrehan (opposite, top) is in Harahan near LaPlace. Built in 1787, it was of French Colonial style but later acquired the Greek Revival colonnade. Below (in Harahan) is Ormond, a pure French Colonial from 1790. The wings were added much later. These are connected to the main house only by galleried passageways that slope down to the main second-floor gallery.

HAHNVILLE - 1801

Home Place (opposite, top) is a beautiful French Colonial plantation house crying for loving care The walls are built of bousillage. Large brick columns support the second-story gallery and the great hip roof is supported, in turn, by slender wood columns centered over those below. The front rooms on both the lower and upper levels open directly onto the galleries, which extend around the house. Transoms over the doors admit air when the doors are closed and shuttered against the sun.

EDGARD - 1807

Glendale (opposite, below) is a Home Place in excellent repair. It, too, is French Colonial but differs from Home Place in minor respects: The roof is higher, with dormers at the ends. There is less difference in the size of the first and second-floor columns. The front gallery stops at the ends of the house rather than turning the corners. The facade is pierced by both windows and doors. Entrance to the second-floor gallery is via steps from the lower gallery and running lengthwise of the house.

WALLACE - 1840

On most plantations at least some of the outbuildings grouped around the main house have disappeared. They are all here at Evergreen (above); and like the house, all have been restored. The twin curving stairways to the raised main floor are unique. Their design is repeated in the layout of the hedges in the front lawn.

NAPOLEONVILLE - 1846

Madewood is pure Greek Revival, pillared outside and in.

The graceful stairs lead to the upper gallery via French doors framed by Corinthian columns. Great sliding doors connect double parlors with marble mantels.

THIBODEAUX - 1796

Rienzi's outside stairs are not quite so lovely as those on Evergreen but are a more integral part of the house and contribute more to its overall beauty, which is considerable. The house (above) is Colonial with classic overtones, especially in the dentiled cornice. The doorways are a bit unusual.

DONALDSONVILLE

Palo Alto is a small, one-and-a-half-story, only slightly raised house with distinct charm. The most noticeable feature of the facade is the sidelights and transom around the door. These are glazed with big bullseyes. The windows also have transoms.

DONALDSONVILLE - 1850

St. Emma's steep hip roof is unusual because the ridge runs from front to back. At the back corner of the house is a circular wing.

VACHERIE - 1839

The enormous Doric columns of Oak Alley contrast with those of St. Emma and Rienzi. Of plastered brick, they rise from ground to roof and are eight feet in circumference. The upper gallery is tied directly into them. They are characteristic of the columns on the Greek Revival mansions of Louisiana. St. Emma's columns, like those of other French Colonial homes, are smaller and in two sections. Large columns support the upper gallery and the roof is supported by smaller columns rising from the gallery floor. More about Oak Alley on the next page.

VACHERIE - 1839

Oak Alley is surrounded by enormous live oaks but not dwarfed by them. Long before the seventy-foot-square house was built, an early settler erected a cottage and planted an allee of twenty-eight oaks down to the Mississippi River a quarter mile distant. This is the allee partially pictured at left, but at the end now stands the massive pink house built by sugar cane.

The house is completely encircled by wide galleries and a total of twenty-eight columns (to match the number of trees). All four sides are alike, even to having three dormers. At the top of the roof is a railed deck for viewing the countryside; but the high levees now hide the river. (Levees also block the river view from other east and west bank homes.)

FRANKLIN - 1837

Oaklawn Manor sits in a huge park-like garden that few Louisiana plantations can equal. But the shining white house takes no back-seat to nature. It is more like the big Greek Revival houses in Natchez than the plantation homes of its own state. In front, at the second-floor level, a balcony with lacy balustrade takes the place of a gallery (but there is a gallery at the rear). The handsome doorways are alike in front and rear. Beyond the back door is a paved terrace with a fountain in the center. Pictured below is the library with marble fireplace.

ST. MARTINVILLE - 1765

The Cajun house in the Longfellow Evangeline State Commemorative Area (above and left) was built by an unusually wealthy Acadian and is bigger than most Cajun homes. Still, it is characteristically simple, free of ornament. The house is raised enough for two rooms on the ground floor. (Most Cajun houses are blocked up only a foot or so—like the French Settlement house at bottom, left.) A zigzag outside stair leads to the rear upper gallery. There are two more rooms at this level and sleeping space under the steep roof. The kitchen is in a separate building. Although the ground floor has brick walls, the walls above are built—as in most Cajun houses—of Spanish-moss-mixed mud sheathed with clapboards.

MANDEVILLE

The Victorian below is within fifty yards of Lake Pontchartrain and the main reason for raising it high was to escape storm damage. That purpose has been achieved. The ornamentation is marvelous; stairs, welcoming.

NEW IBERIA - 1790

The Armand Broussard house (above) was put up by an Acadian. The walls are of bousillage. In typical Cajun fashion, Broussard did not cover the front wall because it is protected from rain by the gallery roof, but he did use siding on the other walls. He strayed from normal practice, however, in using diagonal timbers to brace the walls. Generally—not always—all posts are vertical and spaced close together.

FRANKLIN

Bittersweet (above) is a modified French Colonial house in Greek Revival dress. The French doors are unusual because, instead of folding together, they are separated by a wide framing member. In the Smith house (right) the French doors, hidden behind screens, are conventional. The transoms over the windows are a common feature of Lower Mississippi Valley houses but show up particularly well here.

NEW IBERIA - 1834

Shadows-on-the-Teche is one of the glories of the Lower Mississippi Valley. A town house now owned by the National Trust for Historic Preservation, it is a mixture of French, Spanish, English and Greek Revival styles and from all angles—the front (opposite), the rear, facing Bayou Teche (above), the ends—it's beautiful. It is essentially one room deep for cross ventilation. The stairs to the second floor are in the left end of the galleries and are screened by louvers between the columns (louvers are at the right end of the galleries, too). The ground floor is brick and marble. Marble was used in the dining room (page 140) mainly for practicality, since ground floors used to take a beating from muddy boots.

SHADOWS-ON-THE-TECHE. More on preceding pages.

WASHINGTON - 1826

Although the dormers are a little big for this small plantation house, Home Place is lovely. It is a good example (there are many others in this book) of how well the Greek Revival style could be adapted to small houses. The balustrade swings open at the front steps.

MANSURA

The Dr. Jules Charles des Fosse house is a simple raised French Colonial with surprisingly few openings onto the gallery. The top rails of the balustrade are painted the color of the shutters in contrast to the balusters and bottom rails. This is characteristic of many Valley houses (though the rail color does not always match the trim). I can only guess that it was done so the rails would not show soil so quickly.

ALEXANDRIA - 1800

Originally Kent was a French Colonial with two big, very simple rooms opening onto the upper galleries. The more classic end pavilions were added in 1842. The whole house was recently moved to its present site. The walls of the old part were bousillage; the ground floor was wide open. See a footnote to the text for why the house was raised so high.

SUNSET - 1830

Would that Chretien Point could be seen by every architect and builder in the country. They might learn something about how to make a house beautiful. The brick walls are a pale buff; the plastered brick columns, white. The doors and windows across the front are arched and matching on both gallery levels.

NEW ROADS - 1750

Parlange looked run down for years but by now it is restored to its early beauty. A great gas field on the sugar cane plantation was recently tapped, and when I photographed the house it was crawling with workmen. There is no finer example of the early French-Colonial architectural style; and its charm somehow gains from the fact that the doors onto the galleries are not in nicely balanced rows. The dormers at first appear small for such a huge roof but are in excellent proportion to it. The Parlange family has owned the place from the start.

NEW ROADS

Bonnie Glen (below) is obviously much newer than its ancient neighbor. The attic story, with dormers and gable windows, is exceptionally well ventilated. The big Palladian-style dormer is unusual and practical and adds to the home's appeal.

WHITE CASTLE - 1859

Recently restored Nottoway is the largest extant plantation house in the South. (The only larger one has crumbled.) It has 64 rooms, over 53,000 square feet of space, 200 windows in three full stories. Although the exterior is Italianate, the interiors are essentially Greek Revival. The white ballroom has cypress columns, triple arches, intricate friezes and centerpieces, two white marble mantels, and the original crystal chandeliers. At right is the bedroom of one of the original owners. At far right is the gentleman's study.

CLINTON

The town of Clinton was built by men who must have thought that architecture started and stopped with the Greek Revival style, because it was used in famous Lawyer's Row and everywhere else. Here are two of the oldest and best houses in the town. The Brame-Bennett house (above) dates to 1839. Note the frieze that extends from the front around the sides. The big Marston house (1839) is being restored and one could wish the utilities would assist in the work by removing the maze of cables that mar the facade.

BATON ROUGE

The Florence Coffee house (below) was built in 1850 and is much like houses built in New Orleans' French Quarter in that era. The passageway through the house leads to a courtyard. At the bottom of the page is the Charlet house (1823) in Baton Rouge's Spanish Town. But there's nothing Spanish about the house. It's a simple creole cottage style place with a rear wing that is centered on the main body of the house, forming a T.

BATON ROUGE

The Hart house (above) is a raised one-and-a-half-story Greek Revival dwelling so enveloped by huge magnolias that it cannot be photographed in its entirety. But the doorway is visible and invitingly handsome.

BATON ROUGE

Next to the Charlet house (preceding page) and contrasting sharply to it in size and style is the Stewart-Dougherty house (above), built in 1850 and still owned by the same family (always passing down from mother to daughter). The horizontal openings in the frieze are attic ventilators. The front windows extend to the floor. The dark Chinese Chippendale areas at the window bottoms are screens, and the little squares in the center are tiny doors opening inward so you can put a hand through and pull the shutters closed while indoors.

The Warden's house (right), completed in 1840, is big and not pretty. The kitchen wing is New Orleans style.

BATON ROUGE - 1791

Magnolia Mound is a recently restored plantation house not too far from the center of the city. It is pure French Colonial outside but the interiors are of more classic design. The mantel and chimney breast shown are much ornamented with moldings and panels. The spreading vase-like construction below the ceiling is unusual. Compare with the simple, actually homely, fireplace in the Kent house, which was built at about the same time.

JACKSON

When the middle part of Asphodel (opposite) was built in 1820, there were four rooms on the main floor above the kitchen and two in the attic. In 1833 two-room wings of equal size were added at both ends at the main-floor level. These were connected by an open gallery extending across the back of the old house. In 1949 the gallery was enclosed (bottom, opposite), and in 1958 the ground floor was finished off, thus turning a fine old house into a modern home for a big family. The work, however, was not done without difficulty, because both interior and exterior walls are made of three-course brick; consequently, wires, pipes and ducts were so hard to install that the present owners freely admit they have a hodge-podge heating and cooling system. On the other hand, once the house has reached the right temperature, the thick walls hold it for a long time.

Above, in the center of Jackson, is a wonderful large Greek Revival town house with stucco walls painted a bright peach, white columns and dark green shutters. The first floor is noticeably taller than the second. This is characteristic of Valley houses of this style but just the opposite of raised French Colonial houses.

ST. FRANCISVILLE

Even without the mass of azaleas, the Widow Ross house (above) would delight the eye. It dates from 1850. Virginia (left) was built in sections, starting with the low cottage. When the formal two-story addition was made in 1855, the gallery was built onto the cottage to unify the overall appearance of the house.

ST. FRANCISVILLE - 1831

Ellerslie is like a Greek temple. It sits atop a gentle slope overlooking rolling fields. It was almost the twin of the much photographed Greenwood, not too far away. The huge, slightly hipped roof is supported on the front and sides by great plastered brick columns. The wide upper gallery just touches the columns and is tied into them by timbers (and recently added steel). All windows onto the galleries are jib windows (left). The house has only four rooms and two enormous central halls on each floor. Wide spiral stairs lead all the way to the attic. As in many of the great Valley houses, all hardware is silver-plated.

ST. FRANCISVILLE

Propinquity (top) was built in 1809; acquired a brick wing about twenty years later. The sweeping gable roof is slightly broken just below the ridge but has parapets at each end that make the roof, seen from a gable end, appear straight.

The two-story end of the Camilla Leake Barrow house (middle) dates from 1809. It was a plain New England kind of structure except for the floor-to-ceiling windows and balcony. The semi-saltbox addition was made later, possibly when the one-story Greek Revival wing was built.

The Cottage (bottom) is L-shaped although this is not apparent here. It is 147 feet long. All the rooms in the front wing open onto the gallery.

ST. FRANCISVILLE - 1799

Oakley, alas, is better known because Audubon was employed here to teach the owner's daughter than for itself. It is one of the Valley's most charming vernacular houses. It is almost devoid of ornamentation; appears at one with the surrounding forest. The galleries in front and back are jalousied to keep out sun and rain. Mantels, like that in the dining room with its punkah, are of Adam style.

ST. FRANCISVILLE - 1835

When Rosedown was built in 1835, the rich owners spared nothing in their efforts to make it the most elegant home in the Lower Mississippi Valley; and the present owners followed suit when they restored it about twenty-five years ago. The result is perfection—not only in the house but in the vast park-like gardens, which the first owners planted with rare specimens that long ago attained full size.

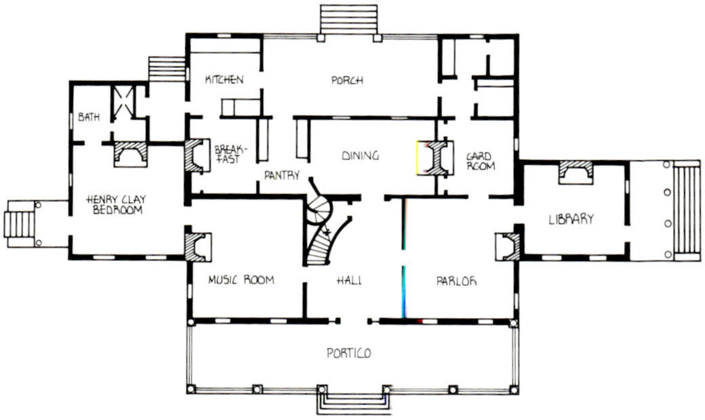
KITCHEN
PORCH
BATH
BREAK-FAST
PANTRY
DINING
CARD ROOM
HENRY CLAY BEDROOM
LIBRARY
MUSIC ROOM
HALL
PARLOR
PORTICO

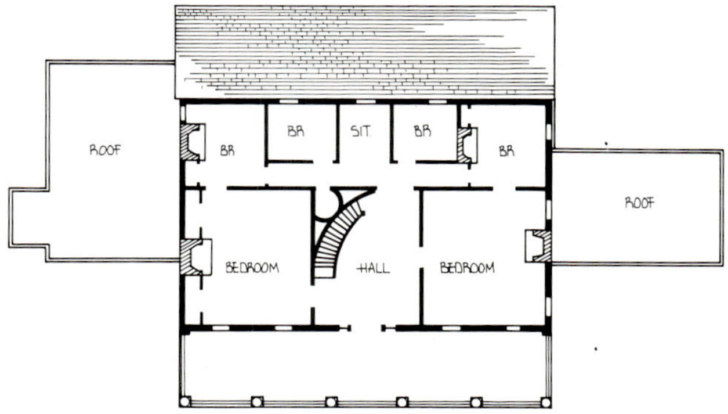
ROOF
BR
BR
SIT
BR
BR
ROOF
BEDROOM
HALL
BEDROOM

NACHITOCHES

The Lemee house (above) stands hard against the sidewalk and looks like nothing to bother with as you pass. But in back it's charming. Built about 1835, it is unusual in that it has a basement. Hardly visible here at the recessed back of the covered patio is the stair to the upper floor. At right is the Tante Hippe house (1835). Unlike the Lemee house, it faces the street, but the owner sought a measure of privacy by installing a gate in the balustrade.

NATCHEZ - 1840

South of Nachitoches many plantations are strung out along the winding Cane River. Oaklawn is one of the first you encounter. The storage of farm equipment in the basement gallery does not detract from the home's beauty.

NACHITOCHES AND VICINITY

The Roque house (above) was built in 1790. It is a tiny, much modified French Colonial house with considerable resemblance to the Black-owned African house on nearby Melrose plantation. It was moved to Nachitoches. The walls are of unfinished bousillage. Opposite are two more of the beautiful French Colonial plantation homes just south of Nachitoches. At top is Cherokee (1820), in the tiny community of Natchez. The other is Oakland (1818), in Bermuda.

Arkansas
1. Altheimer
2. Batesville
3. DeWitt
4. Helena
5. Little Rock
6. Mabelvale
7. Pine Bluff

HELENA

Arkansas was the last of the Lower Mississippi Valley states to be settled and to become a state. Its first permanent settlement was established in 1785. It was admitted to the Union in 1836. It is therefore not surprising that its houses are of more recent vintage than those in the other states.

The Barlow-Coolidge house (above) appears from the street to be smaller than it is. It was built in 1852 and is of obvious Victorian design. The fact that it is raised a couple of feet off the ground indicates no kinship with the French Colonial homes farther south. Almost all houses throughout the country at this time were raised to obviate the need for digging deep basements.

The interior doorway (right) is in the James C. Tappan house pictured on the next page. It is an elaborate design but not unusual for the period. The glass is frosted and elegantly figured. The slightly pyramidal door panels are repeated on the doorway surround above the arch.

HELENA - 1858

The James C. Tappan house is one of Arkansas' best Greek Revival homes though it is slightly tinged with Victorian features. Purists among Revival architects probably frowned on the clapboard walls, because smooth siding, such as flush boards, was preferred. But many houses were like this; and many "proper" Greek Revival houses were not so pretty.

HELENA - 1825

Estevan Hall is an unusual and imposing structure because of its length and because the ground floor extends all the way out to the front of the gallery and is finished as well as the floor above. Note that every opening is arched and the dormer roofs are also arched. Although it's not clear in this picture, the door at the left end of the gallery is flanked by windows and the entire triple opening is surmounted by an arch. The gallery balustrade is iron and has ornamental panels alternating with three straight balusters. The gallery roof at the right end of the house was extended to serve as a carport but the work was done so carefully that it appears to be part of the original house. The parked cars are gradually being screened from the street by shrubbery.

HELENA

The Moore-Horner house (1859) is a large Greek Revival-Victorian hybrid, and it would look very plain if it were not for the ornamental ironwork of the first and second-story porches. But the doorway (above) is lovely and welcoming—as front entrances should be. The Jerome Bonaparte Pillow house (right) is one of those amazing structures that the wealthy in the later 1800s loved to build.

ALTHEIMER - 1866

The Elms is a steep-roofed vernacular Victorian raised house with a gallery that looks as if it were an afterthought. It's an oddly appealing place because of its uncommon decorative features. The chimneys with their elaborate tops are not unusual though they generally rise high above the ridge. The roofs of the dormers suggest a trio of men wearing too-big hats. Actually, because of the roofs, the dormers gain much needed mass: with ordinary small roofs, they would be too skinny and out of proportion with the house. The balustrades do not form a level line; the sections at either end are a few inches higher than those in the middle. The columns appear to be joined by hoops—as they are on two other houses on earlier pages. In this case, however, the hoops are not complete.

DE WITT - 1854

The pleasant Halliburton house has survived a problem that might have wrecked it if it were not of frame construction. The ground in the surrounding eleven-block area has the inexplicable habit of tilting after heavy rains, then returning to normal. The stress this puts on nearby brick houses is more than they can stand.

LITTLE ROCK - 1843

A number of the old homes, large and small, in the Lower Mississippi Valley are no longer homes. In one way this is too bad; in another it isn't, because the people now using them for offices, shops, etc., have often saved them from deterioration—even collapse—and restored them to their original glory. That is what the Junior League did for Trapnall Hall. Today it is a simple but lovely brick building. True, it is of a Greek Revival type that you frequently see in many parts of the United States. But despite its relatively small size, it has an air of distinction, comfort and warmth that makes you stop and wish you could call it your own home.

LITTLE ROCK

The Pike-Fletcher-Terry house is a grand mansion in a park-like setting in the middle of the city. Originally it was more faithful to the Greek Revival style, because the roof was much flatter. This was raised and the dormers, which are definitely not Greek Revival, were installed to provide more living space. The entrance, with its handsome entablature, is guarded by brick columns (the bricks are exposed) with Ionic capitals.

LITTLE ROCK - 1826

The Arkansas Territorial Capitol Restoration preserves in the heart of downtown Little Rock several of the old homes of the early town. The most prominent of these, because it fronts on the sidewalk around the restoration, is the Hinderliter house, which was also the old territorial capitol. On the street side it is a stark white building suggestive of New England except for the shallow roof. But in back it is a galleried southern vernacular house with all the charm such houses have. Under the clapboards are logs.

LITTLE ROCK

The Noland house in the Capitol Restoration (above) was built in the 1830s. It is much like old Virginia homes but the window treatment and doorway are Greek Revival. In back at ground level is a small columned porch overlooking a boxwood-bordered garden. Two small outbuildings are on either side of the garden. Both this house and the Hinderliter house were built on their sites. But the neat one-story framed Conway house (right) was moved to the Restoration. It was built in the 1850s.

MABELVALE - 1828

Ten Mile House is known by several other names and was once an old stage-coach stop. It is splendid proof—if proof is needed—that an ultra-simple house with little ornament can be very beautiful. This beauty is largely attributable to the tall connected chimneys and low sweeping parapets, which are Greek Revival features. The cornice is dentiled.

The house has had a hard time. It was restored some years ago; then it was left unoccupied by its owners and began to fall prey to vandals. Now the owners' children have moved in and started to undo the damage. But because of a vulnerable position close to a well traveled road leading into nearby Little Rock, it will survive and thrive only if guarded with diligence.

LITTLE ROCK

The White-Baucum house, built in the second half of the Nineteenth Century, is a conservative Victorian that anyone —even one who dislikes Victorian—can like. The house was large enough to start with but was later extended by the big wing partly shown at right.

LITTLE ROCK - 1881

Villa Marie is an Italianate Victorian—more elegant than the White-Baucum house and probably not so pleasing to modern tastes, but a fine livable house nonetheless. Despite differences in the sizes and shapes of the windows, the architect tied them all together by giving them pediments of the same design (though in varying shapes).

BATESVILLE

The Glenn house (above), 1850, would be just another big house if it were not for the gable above the portico and the angled (five sides of an octagon) west end. These give it character. As does the color scheme—pale grey with deeper grey shutters and cream-colored trim.

The Garrott house (right) is an 1842 vernacular design with Gothic trim. The prettiest part of the house, which unfortunately was too cluttered to be pictured, is a shallow porch on a stone wing appended to the rear. Below the Gothic trim, the square porch columns are joined by diamond lattice screens with arched openings for passage. It is a charming sitting place.

PINE BLUFF - 1830

The Hudson-Grace-Borreson house began life as a log house; then was remodeled, as you see it, in 1860. What a fanciful job the builder did, especially in the treatment of the dormers on the mansard roof. The house is now a dark red-brown with ivory trim accented in deep brown.

PINE BLUFF

The contrast between the Hudson-Grace-Borreson house on the preceding page and the neighboring Trulock-Gould-Mullis house (1876) is sharp. You might think the latter (above) comes off badly in the comparison; but its lack of flamboyance and gentle charm prevent this. It is enhanced by the comparison and vice versa. At first glance its prettiness seems to stem from the arched door surrounded by arching strips of glass and the triple gable windows. These play an important part, no doubt, but the day is carried by the house's overall indefinable graciousness. Houses of this shape and style—the country is full of them—rarely look so gracious.

DuBocage (right) has the same roofline, the same general style but lacks the Trulock-Gould-Mullis home's subtilty. It's just a big comfortable home. It was constructed ten years earlier.

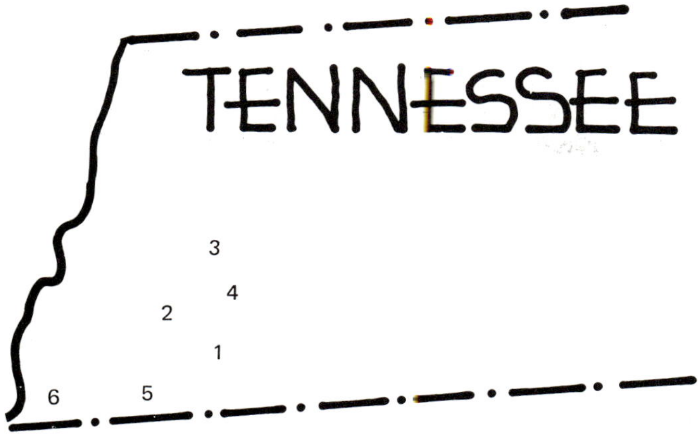

Tennessee
1. Bolivar
2. Brownsville
3. Humboldt
4. Jackson
5. LaGrange
6. Memphis

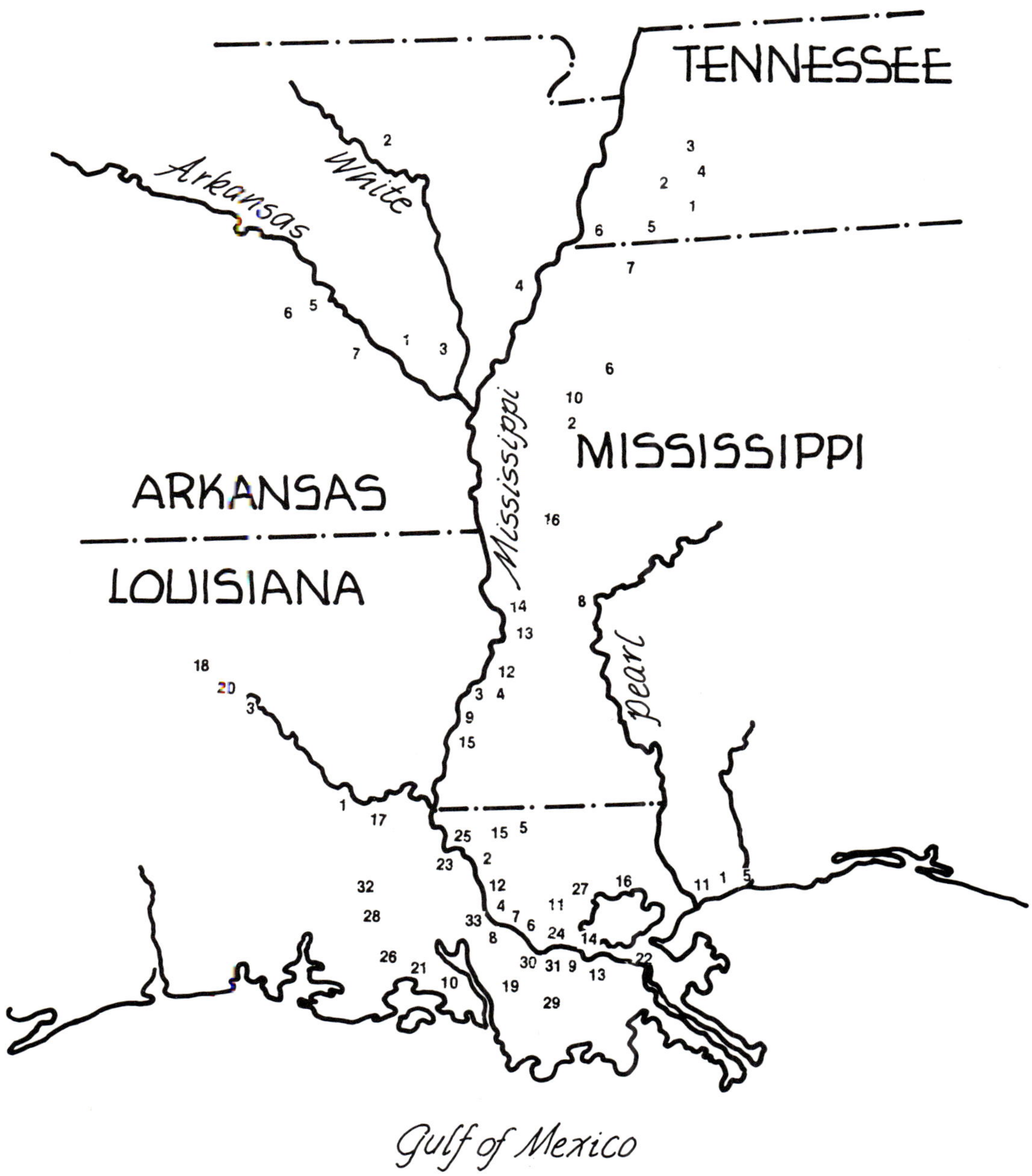

JACKSON

The DeBerry-Hurt house, a big, rather severe, Virginia-style country home, was being completely overhauled when I saw it. Without a porch, the fanlighted front door was lonesome yet still attractive. It is unusually narrow for the entrance to a Mississippi Valley house.

HUMBOLDT

In the first half of the Nineteenth Century, many houses in the northern reaches of the Valley, and elsewhere in the South, were tall and skinny like that at right—partly because one-room-deep houses were then traditional, partly to improve ventilation.

HUMBOLDT

The houses on these two pages are quite typical of early Tennessee architecture. Greek Revival was in vogue. The white house opposite is a fine example, though Revival purists would probably prefer that it had smooth siding and would almost surely object to the Gothic sidelights.

MEMPHIS

The ever-so-attractive Greek Revival home below is sandwiched between great mansions. It deserves a more isolated site. Built about 1840, it has a wide center hall, two big front rooms with two smaller ones behind. Each room in each pair has a fireplace. The huge Ramsay house (right) lorded over a plantation when built and was much smaller, the wings having been added. The original central block had the general outlines of a Greek Revival structure but largely lacked the typical detailing.

MEMPHIS - 1870

The Lee house (above) and Fontaine house (right) are the two finest examples of the Victorian style in Memphis. They were built at the same time and are within a stone's throw of each other. To us today they seem hideously big and overly ornamented; but as Victorian mansions went, they were quite restrained. The detailing is superb. Children growing up in both houses must have had a field day —if their elders were not too strict.

MEMPHIS

Memphis abounds in houses like these (as do many other cities). Most have elaborate over-window and door treatments and heavy bracketed cornices like those on this page. They are a pleasure to look at for these reasons. The Bradford-Maydwell house opposite is of the same mid-Nineteenth Century vintage but considerably more restrained. It is a spot of beauty in a terribly drab neighborhood and one can only hope it will escape "progress".

648

MEMPHIS

More of Memphis's best. Like the house on the preceding page, that below, right is fairly conservative. But the two other houses are good examples of the Italianate style that flourished in the Victorian era. The brackets supporting the cornices are large and heavily molded, and they were used in pairs as they often—but not always—were. The window surrounds are incredible and all were handcrafted (stock materials were available in the latter half of the Nineteenth Century but not in such elaborate forms as these). The quoins are bold. The division between floors is indicated by the horizontal coursing. For practicality, both houses have large openings below the cornice to ventilate and partially light the low attics.

MEMPHIS - 1836

The little Magevney house, in the shadow of the city's largest buildings, is the oldest house in Memphis. It looks like many of the early small homes in Virginia—a simple white-clapboard place with a steep gable roof. The original house had two downstairs rooms, each with an end fireplace. The low rear wing was added. The chimneys have an elegant Virginia flair although the corbelled enlargement at the top is unusually squat.

MEMPHIS

Up and down the Valley the ceiling centerpieces almost make you wish you had high ceilings, too. This exceptionally ornate piece and the intricately painted ceiling are in the Mallory-Neely house.

MEMPHIS - 1852

When it was put up, the Mosby-Bennett house was a vernacular plantation home somewhat influenced by the Greek Revival style. The features of the old style remain, but when the house was remodeled in the 1870s, they were obscured to some degree by Victorian ornamentation—the bargeboards on the end gables, scrollwork above the windows and the peak of the central gable, bracketed and chamfered porch posts, the fancy balustrades. Just two years ago the house was remodeled again, but this time mainly to redesign the interior (while preserving the past) for the real estate firm that is now the owner.

LA GRANGE

From the housing standpoint, little LaGrange is western Tennessee's gem, although the houses all tend to be sizable, white-painted frame structures of the same general character. There are lots of them. Tiara (above) is reasonably typical. It was built in 1845. Chantilly, right, dates from 1850. It is smaller, more Victorian and unusually well landscaped.

LA GRANGE

Westover of Woodstock is most closely associated with Lucy P. Holcombe Pickens, the only woman whose likeness has appeared on American paper currency (Confederate currency). But neither Lucy nor her family can rightfully put the Pickens name on the house, because they bought it in 1832. At that time it was already known as an old house; the previous owner's name was not recorded in the deed. In any event, it was a big, handsome Federal home (see next page, too).

Eventually it was abandoned, and when the present owners purchased it, it was falling completely apart and terribly overgrown. Happily, it is now in the process of being restored to its early beauty although not exactly to its early form, because a dilapidated gallery across the front was removed and the equally dilapidated rear wing that gave the house an L shape has been replaced by a new wing in a T shape. But among many other things, the twin doorways and parlor fireplace are original. And despite the suggestion of the current owners' architect that windows should be installed, the "blind ends" of the house have been retained because they were characteristic of Federal homes of this type.

LA GRANGE

Above is Westover of Woodstock. On the facing page, at top, is nearby Woodlawn, on a hilltop overlooking surrounding fields. It was built in 1828. Though closely akin to plantation houses farther south, I know of none other like it in western Tennessee.

BOLIVAR - 1869

The house opposite, bottom, is called the Presbyterian Manse and it looks just as the manse in a small town ought to look. It's a typical Victorian cottage of the kind that Andrew Jackson Downing advocated: tall chimneys, steep, broken roof, Gothic-arched windows, fancy trim.

BOLIVAR

The 1869 house above resembles a Natchez town house of the same era. Once more we see hoop-like arches between the porch columns, but these are heavier and more elaborate than earlier specimens. On the opposite page are two substantial, handsome Greek Revival homes. The two-story portico with triple corner columns and high entablature is unusually massive.

BROWNSVILLE

A nice entrance and fine frieze mark the unpretentious, friendly little hip-roofed, brick house below.

Missouri and Illinois

1. Cahokia
2. Clayton
3. Crestwood
4. Fredericksburg
5. Gasconade County
6. Hazelwood
7. Kaskaskia
8. Perryville
9. St. Charles
10. Ste. Genevieve
11. St. Louis
12. Washington
13. Webster Groves
14. Westphalia

ST. LOUIS - 1851

The Campbell house in the heart of downtown is a towering spreading Italianate-tinged home that has become a museum furnished and decorated as it was in the 1860s. The intriguing structure at left is a covered walk to a thoroughly delightful gazebo. Beyond this, just visible, is the large carriage house.

ST. LOUIS - 1840

The Henry Shaw town house was moved from downtown St. Louis and is now connected to the offices of the Missouri Botanical Garden. Shaw's even bigger Tower Grove house is also in the garden. The town house is as conservative in design inside as out. The drawing room fireplace (above) is one of its few elaborate features.

CRESTWOOD - 1808

When Thomas J. Sappington built this house with adjacent outbuildings, he may have been recalling homes he knew in Virginia and Maryland, because it bears a strong resemblance to them. There are few if any like it in the Lower Mississippi Valley.

ST. LOUIS - 1854

Unlike other states in the Valley, Missouri has ample stone for building so it's interesting that more houses are not built of it. Even if they were, none could quite equal magnificent Oakland.

WEBSTER GROVES - 1857

The Hawken house looks like hundreds of others in the South and elsewhere when you approach it (left); but when you get around in back you are suddenly in the Mississippi Valley. The one unanswered question is why the galleried wing looks as if it had been split down the middle. Architecturally, the interior is as simple as the wing. Fireplaces provided heat in some rooms; stoves, in others.

The house is unusual in that it has closets. Closets were virtually unheard of in the Valley (armoires were used instead), because starting with the early Spanish governors, they were taxed as rooms. Hawken tried to get around the assessors—and evidently did—by eliminating closet doorknobs. The doors have keyholes only. The interior pictures and floor plans are overleaf.

HAWKEN HOUSE. More on preceding page.

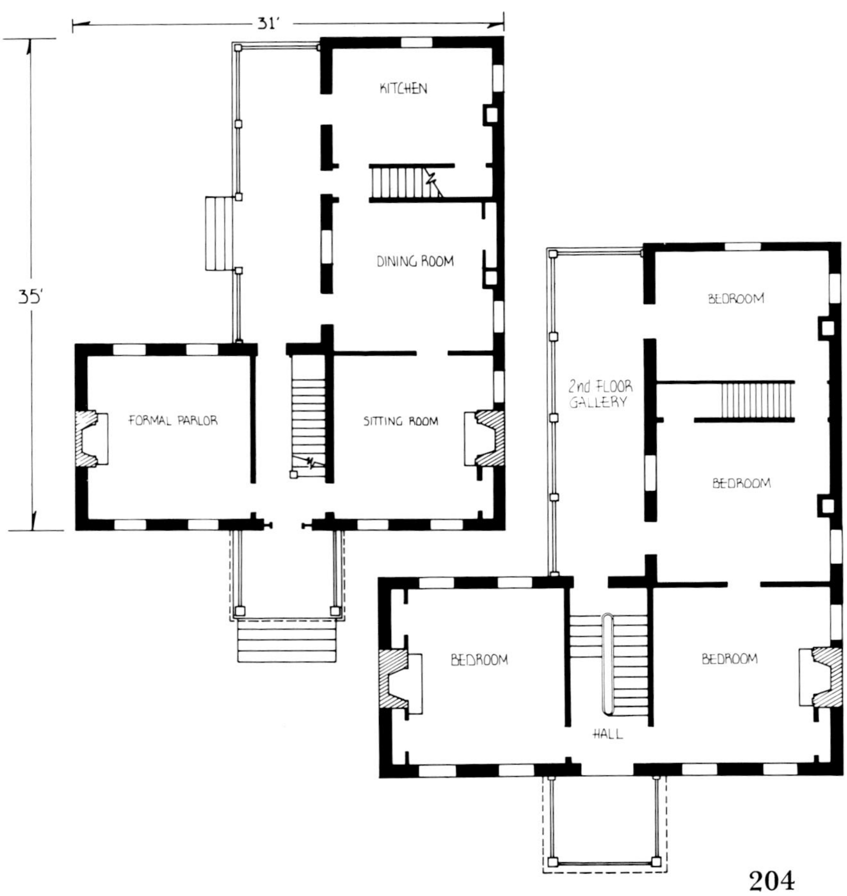

CLAYTON - 1855

The Martin Franklin Hanley house (above) was the home of a successful farmer. The Greek Revival design is typical of the area.

HAZELWOOD - 1800

The Utz-Tesson home (right) was also a farmhouse. The gallery columns are in two sections—square below; smaller and chamfered above.

ST. CHARLES

Second Street in St. Charles is a street of utter delight. The houses that front on it date to the very early 1800s, when the town was the capital city of Missouri. It's true that most of the houses are now stores inviting the tourist. But there's a paucity of signs to indicate this. If you could remove the automobiles and utility lines, you'd be back in early days.

The old houses in the black and white photo comprise Stone Row.

PERRYVILLE

The neat little house above with galleries stuck on fore and aft now belongs to the Perry County Historical Society. Note that the chimneys are inside the end walls rather than outside as in most Southern houses. The brick and stone construction is unusual and indicates the house was built in sections. At right is the Shelby-Nicholson-Schwindler house built in 1860.

FREDERICKBURG - 1859

This stone house was built by people of German descent who came to Missouri from the East. We may assume they knew little about early construction in the deep South (though they may have been influenced by houses in Ste. Genevieve). Yet note the general similarity of this house to old houses way down the Mississippi—the result of the environment. The house has galleries and is one room deep for summer comfort. It was raised—very high—on stout stone columns so it would not be flooded by the nearby river. The second floor is reached by outside stairs. Despite the simplicity of the structure, the builder went to the trouble of arching the doorway.

WASHINGTON - 1850

The Augustus W. Krueger house (above) is a localized Greek Revival structure that at one time had a front porch and entrance (the new entrance is sad). One of the most imposing houses in town, it has a third floor under the shallow roof. It probably does not have side windows because there was another sizable house next door. The spiral stair (opposite) is in the house. Note that, despite the pretentiousness of the house, the stairs do not have scrolls on the stringer.

GASCONADE COUNTY - 1858

In smaller houses along the lower Missouri River, the stairs were commonly boxed in as at left—indicating that the first floor was heated, the second was not. Even outside stairs to second floors were sometimes enclosed.

WESTPHALIA - 1840

A roof that sweeps out over a first-floor gallery always has a special charm. And when it's a long, low house with a slight curve in the roof—as in the Westermann home—the effect is even greater. This was a log house. The walls were covered with clapboards in rather recent times.

CAHOKIA, ILLINOIS - 1738

Floods took early Cahokia. There were only a dozen or so residents of the town when the Capt. Jean Baptiste Saucier house was built. It is the oldest house in Illinois, probably the oldest in the Lower Mississippi Valley, and it is a perfect example of the French Colonial architectural style—which in this case came from Canada with the French missionaries. The walls are made of squared posts resting on a sill on stone foundations. The spaces between posts are filled with stone and mortar. This is the *poteaux-sur-solle* construction method.

The house, now with four rooms (it probably had two at the start) became a courthouse in 1793. It was moved to the St. Louis world's fair in 1904; then to Chicago. It was returned to Cahokia in 1938 and is state owned.

KASKASKIA, ILLINOIS - 1800

The Pierre Menard house was built long after the original settlement was destroyed. A typical French Colonial, it would be quite at home in Louisiana but, like the Saucier house, owes its design to the men who settled in Canada.

STE. GENEVIEVE - 1785

The famous Bolduc house is not the oldest in Ste. Genevieve but most accurately portrays the French Colonial style. Including the galleries, it is 82 by 48 feet. It is raised above ground. The walls are made of oak timbers set on a stone foundation, with bousillage between posts. Interior walls are rough plaster. Inside and out the house is whitewashed. The steep hip roof is supported by oak trusses like those used in Normandy. The restoration of the first kitchen behind the house is shown at right. In 1820 the back gallery was partly enclosed for a new kitchen. More on next pages.

BOLDUC HOUSE

The Bolduc house is essentially two big rooms and a central hall (shown from front door, above). The bedroom is to the left of the hall. The living-dining room (opposite, top) was on the other side of the hall and the new kitchen with alcove (both at bottom) was on the rear gallery. The fireplaces with oak lintels were enormous. The attic floor was supported on great beams. More on preceding page.

STE. GENEVIEVE - 1784

The Guibord-Valle house stands close to the street (like most of the town's houses). The long gallery is approached from either end and the house, like some others, has two front doors. A rear gallery facing a lovely walled garden has been enclosed. The house is of *poteaux-sur-solle* construction.

The roofs of most of Ste. Genevieve's ancient French Colonials were originally hipped. They were converted into gable roofs to make the attics more livable. This may or may not have been done here. But the Norman trusses illustrated on the facing page are original and are typical of this architectural style. Like the modern truss, these form an A, but there the similarity ends. The center posts, rising from the chords (or cross girts) extend above the A's and support the ridge timber. The ridge is also supported by V-forming diagonals, mortised into the posts and running parallel with the ridge. Diagonals and posts are tied together with an intermediate timber under the ridge. Purlins (timbers that also parallel the ridge) are notched into the sides of the A's, and the rafters rest on these so that there are open spaces between the roof sheathing and the trusses. The entire massive structure is fastened together by a system of mortised and lapped joints, each secured by large pegs.

STE. GENEVIEVE - 1787

Even though defaced by utility lines, the Jean Baptiste Valle house is one of the most appealing in the entire Lower Mississippi Valley. Its history is confused, but there is little doubt that the basement was once a fort with buttressed stone walls up to four feet thick. The house itself is of bousillage construction, and although the exterior walls have not been changed, many other things have been. Rooms have been added and the roof has been extensively modified.

Like so many Ste. Genevieve homes, the Valle property is surrounded by a high solid fence. This is a throwback to early days.

STE. GENEVIEVE

If all of Ste. Genevieve's homes were of French Colonial design, the town would tend to seem monotonous. Obviously, since the town has been in existence since the early Eighteenth Century and has slowly grown, there have been many architectural changes that help to point up the beauty of the early style. Many of these newer houses are also interesting in their own right. For example, the Charles Hertich house (below) is a most attractive vernacular version of the Victorian era's Second Empire style, which was characterized by the mansard roof. It was built in 1850. The Simon Hubardeau house (opposite) is a stark limestone structure softened by a white clapboarded addition (only the roof shows). It dates from 1789.

STE. GENEVIEVE

The Bequette-Ribault house (1775), left, and the Beauvais house (1770) were built by the *poteaux-en-terre* method illustrated in the large picture. Heavy posts were sunk into the ground and stone and mortar were crammed between them. The Bequette-Ribault house, now being restored, probably had a hip roof and galleries on all four sides. The Beauvais house was built on *le grand champ*. It was moved to its present site in 1790 and has been much altered.

STE. GENEVIEVE - 1818

The Felix Valle home (opposite) is a lovely stone vernacular house with Georgian doorway and dentiled cornice. The house originally had a stoop; later the doorway with its arched surround was recessed. A saltbox addition, not clearly visible here, was added. The tiny windows flanking the big upper-story windows are reminiscent of the arrangement in Cape Cod houses (though the builder is not known to have been connected with New England).

STE. GENEVIEVE - 1805

Linden was originally a two-room house of *poteaux-sur-solle* construction. It was enlarged some time after 1860 by a big galleried wing extending back from the right rear corner. The overly large dormers were probably added at the same time.

STE. GENEVIEVE - 1770

The St. Gemme-Amoureux house is the subject of conjecture and debate. It may have been moved to high ground after the 1785 flood. It may have been—and probably was—considerably longer. And it may not have acquired (and probably did not) its gallery until after 1800. But no one questions its French origin. It was built by the *poteaux-en-terre* method and had a thatched roof. A very steep stair at the left end of the gallery permitted rather difficult access to the attic.

STE. GENEVIEVE - 1802

The Janis-Ziegler house, more commonly known as the Green Tree Tavern, is a raised house encircled by galleries. Its kinship with other French Colonial houses in Ste. Genevieve is obvious; but unlike the other houses of its age, it has American rather than Norman roof trusses. A central chimney serves three fireplaces—one in the parlor and one in each of the two bedrooms adjoining. The latter two are set at an angle to the former, creating a triangle resting on a triangular foundation.

STE. GENEVIEVE - 1820

The Bolduc-LeMeilleur house has gone through trying times. You see it on the opposite page as it is today and as it was long ago. But at one time it was connected by a passageway to a nearby brick building (which was later extended all the way to the house). And in about 1850 it was turned into a two-story hotel. It was restored to a simple story-and-a-half house with front and rear galleries only a few years ago. The windows are set very high instead of on a level with the door heads.

STE. GENEVIEVE - 1795

The Mammy Shaw house, left, bears little resemblance to the French Colonial homes of Ste. Genevieve and may have been built later than the indicated date. It first had only one big room but was divided and expanded in 1852. At that time three doors from the pilothouse of a wrecked steamboat were used to separate living room from bedroom. There is also an ornamental cutglass door from the same ship. Despite these refinements, the house still shows its early days in the adz marks on the beams and plane marks on the ceiling boards.

INDEX